The Observers Series
SHIPS

About the Book

This pocket guide contains information on numerous types of ships—merchant ships, car ferries, cruise ships, fishing vessels, warships and sailing ships. The shipping industry is constantly changing; new types of vessels appear as others lose their importance. In this revised edition the text has been thoroughly updated to deal with such developments as short-sea and oceangoing container ships, car carriers, the use of nuclear power, and a study of sailing-ships for possible re-introduction as cargo carriers.

There are descriptions of ensigns, flags and signals, and the text is also illustrated with many line drawings and black and white photographs.

About the Author

The author was educated at Buxton College and Manchester College of Art, pursuing a career as art teacher and lecturer, and as head of a department at Bournemouth College of Art. He served in the RAF as an interpreter of Air Photographs (shipping and port installations) with some lecturing to Coastal Command aircrews on ship recognition. His publications include *Merchant Ship Recognition* (for service use), *Ships of the Cunard Line* and handbooks on lettering. For many years he was on the panel of lecturers for the Scottish Arts Council and his topics included *Ships' Figureheads* and *Marine Painting*.

The *Observer's* series was launched in 1937 with the publication of *The Observer's Book of Birds*. Today, over fifty years later, paperback *Observers* continue to offer practical, useful information on a wide range of subjects, and with every book regularly revised by experts, the facts are right up-to-date. Students, amateur enthusiasts and professional organisations alike will find the latest *Observers* invaluable.

'Thick and glossy, briskly informative' – *The Guardian*

'If you are a serious spotter of any of the things the series deals with, the books must be indispensable' – *The Times Educational Supplement*

O B S E R V E R S

SHIPS

Frank Dodman

FREDERICK WARNE

FREDERICK WARNE
Published by the Penguin Group
27 Wrights Lane, London W8 5TZ, England
Viking Penguin Inc., 40 West 23rd Street, New York, New York 10010, U.S.A.
Penguin Books Australia Ltd, Ringwood, Victoria, Australia
Penguin Books Canada Ltd, 2801 John Street, Markham, Ontario, Canada L3R 1B4
Penguin Books (N.Z.) Ltd, 182–190 Wairau Road, Auckland 10, New Zealand

Penguin Books Ltd, Registered Offices: Harmondsworth, Middlesex, England

First published 1973
New editions 1981, 1986
Reprinted 1987, 1990 (with revisions)
Copyright © Frederick Warne & Co., 1973, 1981, 1986
Originally published as *The Observer's Book of*
Ships in small hardback format

Acknowledgement
The author and publishers are grateful to the copyright holders who
have kindly provided photographs.

All the line drawings and unacknowledged
photographs are by the author.

Library of Congress Catalog Card No 73 80246

ISBN 0 7232 3708 5

Printed and bound in Great Britain by
William Clowes Limited, Beccles and London

CONTENTS

PREFACE

The main purpose of this book is to introduce the observer to the wide variety of vessels existing today under the four main headings— *merchant ships* and their auxiliaries such as tugs; *warships* and their non-combatant auxiliaries; *fishing vessels*; and *sail training vessels*. It also aims at providing some general background about ships and the sea. In recent years some new types have appeared which do not quite fit into the main categories. These, like the oil rig supply vessel and the semi-submersible heavy-lift carrier, are associated with the new offshore oil industry. The container (or box) ship still dominates the freight trade and 'super' container ships are appearing; the sea-going general cargo break-bulk carrier is being replaced by the multi-purpose combination carrier which incorporates facilities for containers. The days of the giant tanker seem to be nearly over as so many of them are either laid up or are now being scrapped.

Approximately 200 passenger liners operate the cruise market; many of these are recently purpose-built vessels, and several more will be launched in the coming years. In the 1990s new 50,000 gt cruise liners will be in operation, to be surpassed by a ship capable of carrying 2,500 passengers; and if, and when, the projected 210,000 gt ship is built she will carry twice that number of cruise passengers. Sail-assisted motor power is getting beyond the experimental stage and the latest such vessel is a French-built cruise liner for the USA which will have a cruise liner superstructure with a clipper bow, a length of about 133 metres and four masts with five huge triangular sails.

The world-wide cruising market seems to be expanding, but the same is not true about the British shipping scene. Only 10 years ago UK registered ships numbered about 1,600, but that figure has now dropped to about 600; many shipping companies, household names for generations, have either ceased to exist or now operate only a few ships. Extensive road transport has almost killed the coastal trade, but what is left is carried by too many foreign flag vessels.

In a book of this type information comes from many diverse sources, but special mention should be made of the publications of the World Ship Society and its invaluable monthly *Marine News*. Acknowledgement is due to *Jane's Fighting Ships*; to the Ministry of Defence (Navy); to the US Department of the Navy in Washington; and to the Naval Attachés in London of France, Italy and Sweden for information and photographs. Thanks are also due to the Controller of HM Stationery Office for his continuing permission to reproduce flags and a selection of signals from the International Code of Signals (1969). Thanks are due to the many shipping companies who have provided information and photographs, in particular P & O Cruises Ltd, Sealink British Ferries, Norwegian Caribbean Lines, Royal Caribbean Cruise Line, Swedish State Railways, DFDS Seaways and Geest Shipping Division. Over the years many individuals have made helpful suggestions and they are again thanked for their contributions. In connection with this edition, special thanks are due to Philip E. Neumann, director of FotoFlite for his cooperation and excellent photographs of shipping in the English Channel, and to Jim Prentice for supplying photographs from his comprehensive collection; to D. H. Howard of Blue Star Line Ltd; and to P. W. Ridgway of Trinity House Lighthouse Service. Readers with a more particular interest in fighting ships are recommended to consult Hugh W. Cowin's *Warships* in this Observers series.

Fig. 1 Cunard passenger and cruise liner *Queen Elizabeth 2*, now with red and black funnel and luxury penthouses on the uppermost deck

Fig. 2 The P & O Passenger Division's 17,000-ton cruise liner, *Sun Princess*. (ex *Spirit of London*) *By courtesy of P & O*

1 GENERAL INFORMATION Part I
INTRODUCTION

The observer's powers of observation, and his knowledge of ships, generally pass through the following stages:

(*a*) Recognition of the main *groups*: merchant ships, warships, fishing vessels, pleasure craft, sailing vessels, harbour craft.

(*b*) Recognition of the main *types* within these groups, so that he knows the difference between a passenger liner and a cargo liner, a cruiser and a destroyer, a trawler and a drifter.

(*c*) Recognition of the *varieties* within each type—the difference between a fruit carrier and a fast cargo liner, a guided missile destroyer and an anti-submarine destroyer, a barquentine and a topsail schooner.

With his expanding knowledge of types he acquires skill in estimating the *tonnage*, *length* and *speed* of most ships that he sees. At a later stage, by the hull form, funnel shape and character of superstructure he can estimate the approximate *date of building*.

An experienced observer knows many *individual* ships and can state their owners, nationality, tonnage, speed and service, although new vessels now tend to lack company or national characteristics and look very much alike.

In a pocket book of this size there is no space for merchant, naval and fishing fleet lists, but the illustrations and notes provide information on many aspects of ships which will be of service to the observer who pursues his interest in the docks, along the shore, at sea—or even from the air.

Fig. 3 Some nautical terms

Nautical Terms

Abaft Towards the ship's stern. **Abeam** In a line at right angles to the ship's length. Abreast. **Aft** Towards the ship's stern. **Ahead** In advance of the ship's bows. **Amidships** Near the centre of the ship's length. **Astern** Behind the ship. **Athwartships** From one side of the ship to another. **Athwart** Transversely. **Awash** Level with the surface of the water. **Aweigh** Anchor just raised from the sea-bed. **Beam** Greatest breadth of the ship. **Bows** Foremost part of a ship. **Cable** or **cable-length** One-tenth of a nautical mile, 185·2 m (600 ft) or 100 fathoms. **Camber** Athwartship upward curve of a ship's deck. **Fathom** One-hundredth part of a cable (1·82 m or 6 ft). **Flare** or **Flam** The outward and upward curve of a ship's side at the bows. **Forward** Towards the bows. **Knot** Unit of speed. A nautical mile traversed in one hour. **Leeward** Direction to which the wind is blowing. **Lee** Sheltered side away from the wind. **Nautical Mile** One minute of latitude at the equator. Mean nautical mile = 1,852 m. Ten cables. **Port** Left-hand side when looking towards the bows. Earlier known as **larboard. Quarter** Direction between *abeam* and *astern* and that part of a vessel's sides near the stern. **Rake** Slope of a funnel, masts or stem. **Sheer** Fore-and-aft curve of a hull or deck, rising towards bows and stern. **Starboard** Right-hand side when looking towards the bows. **Trim** Way a vessel sits in the water, i.e. on an even keel, down by the head, or down by the stern. **Tumblehome** Upward and inward curve of a vessel's side. **Wake** Foamy water left in track of a ship. **Way** and **Under way** Passage of a ship through the water. **Windward** Direction from which the wind is blowing.

Tonnage

Ship tonnage sometimes confuses the layman, particularly when he finds that one ship can have five different figures, the highest often three times larger than the lowest. Any comparison between tonnage figures must obviously refer to the same sort of tonnage for each of the ships concerned. It is important to distinguish between the two terms *tons* and *tonnes*; the former refers to cubic capacity and the latter to weight in metric tonnes. With regard to merchant ships, *gross*, *net* and *deadweight* tonnage figures are normally used. There is no hard-and-fast relationship between these figures and, unless the ships are of the same type with the same functions, comparisons are apt to be misleading. Tonnage measured by capacity is based on the international unit of 100 ft^3, or 2·83 m^3 equal to one ton.

New international regulations came into force in 1982 and shipowners were given about 12 years to re-measure the gross and net tonnage of their vessels.

Gross registered tonnage (g.r.t. or gt) is the total of all permanently enclosed space above and below decks, with certain exceptions such as the wheelhouse, chart room, radio room, galley, washing facilities and other specified spaces above deck.

Net registered tonnage (n.r.t.) is the earning space of the ship, i.e. the gross tonnage less the crew's accommodation, steering gear and anchor working space, workshops, ballast tanks and machinery space. Gross tonnage is now becoming the basis for harbour dues. Certain ships are classified as open/closed shelter deck vessels (see page 30). The triangular tonnage mark indicates that certain modified or alternative tonnages have been assigned to the ship.

Fig. 4
Plimsoll or
International
Convention
Loadlines and
Tonnage Mark

Tonnage by weight is the weight of water displaced by the vessel. **Light displacement** is the weight of the ship's hull, engines, spares and other items necessary for her working. **Load displacement** is the ship's weight when fully laden, i.e. hull, engines, cargo, crew and everything on board sinking her down to the summer draught loadline. **Deadweight** (d.w. or dwt) is the difference between *light* and *load* displacement and therefore gives the weight—in metric tonnes—of the cargo, ballast, fresh water, fuel, crew and passengers.

Displacement tonnages are calculated in relation to draught and the statutory freeboard which must be shown on the ship's side along with the above markings (**Fig. 4**). Above the latter is a short horizontal line giving the level of the vessel's deck line; the difference between that and the line through the circle is the freeboard. On the grid the letters signify: LR Lloyd's register (the assigning authority), TF Tropical Fresh Water, F Fresh Water, T Tropical Salt Water, S Summer Salt Water, W Winter Salt Water and WNA Winter North Atlantic. These loading marks allow for the different specific gravities; with the same cargo, a ship will sink deeper into the water in seas near the equator than she will in the North Atlantic, in winter.

Methods of Mechanical Propulsion

Steam reciprocating engines The first passenger steamship was the *Comet* of 1812, propelled by a simple 4-h.p. engine driving at first two pairs of paddles, and later one. Fuel consumption was large and consequently her trips were short; all early steamships suffered from the handicap of excessive fuel consumption. The simple engine developed into the two-cylinder compound engine and eventually became the triple-expansion compound engine. The latter was slow, but economical and reliable, and although it was the only method of driving paddles and propellers for nearly a hundred years, it is used now only in a few tugs, spoil hoppers and the older dredgers, and a few preserved steamships. Steam is generated in Scotch fire-tube boilers, passes through a small high-pressure cylinder, a medium-pressure and then, the largest, low-pressure cylinder. A number of coal, and oil-burning steam ferries still operate across the Bosphorus from Istanbul.

Steam reaction turbines Acting on a principle similar to that of the water-wheel, the steam—generated in water-tube boilers—passes through numerous fine nozzles onto small blades fixed round the rim of a cylinder, thus forcing it to revolve. The average turbine revolves at a speed of about 4,000 r.p.m. and before this power can be transmitted to the propeller shaft the rotational speed must be reduced through single, or double, reduction gearing down to about 100 r.p.m. This mechanically simple type of engine is efficient, quiet and smooth running, but with increasing fuel costs its use for merchant ships is diminishing and some modern container ships are now being re-engined with diesel motors.

Electric propulsion is used when the shafts are connected to electric motors for which the current is provided by either steam turbo- or diesel-driven generators. Two outstanding examples are the P & O cruise liner *Canberra* and, after her 1987 refit, Cunard's *Queen Elizabeth 2*. The latter has two electric propulsion motors and nine diesel generating sets.

Diesel motors   The general principle of the marine engine is similar to that of the motor-car internal combustion engine except that the oil fuel is ignited by compression. Compared with the steam engine the fuel consumption is low, and the fact that no fuel is consumed at all when the ship is in port is an advantage. This type of engine is now common for every type of merchant ship.

Gas turbines   Free piston gas turbines were introduced in the late 1950s after a number of experiments in ocean-going ships. The principle is similar to that of the steam turbine but the hot gas provides the motive force to the blades—direct rotary action. In some power installations part of the power is provided by diesel engines, and the gas exhaust from these operates a gas turbine to give additional power. The system is very reliable, easy to maintain and takes up comparatively little space. An increasing number of warships are now propelled by this method, while others have combined systems such as COSOG—steam and gas or CODOG—diesel engines and gas turbine according to the type of ship.

Nuclear reactors   In this new type of marine propulsion a nuclear heat-productivity unit provides steam for conventional low-pressure turbines. The most important advantage is that, using a very small amount of fuel, the vessel can remain at sea for many months without refuelling. This is of great value to the warship, and in particular to the submarine, and the system has therefore first come into general use in submarines. The United States navy does however possess nuclear-powered ships in nearly every important category. Nuclear power units are extremely

Fig. 5
Kort
nozzle

expensive and, as a result, very few merchant ships have been operated with this form of propulsion. The American cargo passenger liner *Savannah* (1954) was the first nuclear-powered commercial vessel, for many years serving as an ocean-going experimental laboratory for the marine reactor. The German nuclear-powered *Otto Hahn* of 1968 was, in 1982, converted to a conventional motor container-ship. The Russian icebreaker *Lenin* and the Japanese *Mutsu* are nuclear-powered vessels.

Changes in methods of propulsion have not been confined to power units; other developments have contributed to greater manoeuvrability and more economical use of fuel. In the **Kort nozzle (Fig. 5)** unit the propeller, shrouded by a short open-ended cylinder, increases pushing power by about 25 per cent, with a consequent saving in fuel costs. If vanes of aerofoil section are fitted, the normal rudder can be dispensed with. This unit reduces vibration and gives better control so that a vessel can turn in a very tight circle; it is mainly used by fishing vessels and tugs.

The **controllable pitch propeller** has 3 or 4 blades, each one of which can turn on its own axis to give greater efficiency under varying conditions and has the advantage that, when going astern, the rotation of the propeller shaft is not reversed.

Many ships of all types and sizes are now equipped with a **bow thruster unit** in which a reversible propeller is situated in a transverse tunnel passing through the hull near the bows. This propeller forces water to one side or the other, as required, and greatly assists movements in docks.

The **Voith-Schneider** cycloidal propeller works rather like a feathered paddle-wheel placed on a vertical instead of a horizontal axis in the bottom of the vessel's hull. Spade-shaped blades project from near the edge of a disc which rotates on a vertical axis; by changing the relative angle of the blades the thrust can be exerted in any direction without the use of a rudder. This type of unit is particularly successful in shallow and confined waters.

The **bulbous bow** reduces pitching, and for tankers and freighters it increases speed when they are sailing in ballast. **Stabilizers** are projecting fins, fitted to passenger ships below the water-line, to reduce the effect of rolling in rough weather.

Fig. 6
Bulbous
bow

Basic Hull Forms, Stems and Sterns

Fig. 7 Basic hull forms, stems and sterns

radar scanner

mainmast

poop

wheelhouse
sidelight
lower bridge
boat deck

stores davit

lifeboat

capstan

hatchway

accommodation

hance

tween decks

stern

aft
peak
w.b.

no 5 hold

main
engine

rudder
propeller (screw)

truck

double bottom - water ballast
fuel oil or fresh water

topmast

crosstrees

5·tonne derricks

forestay

forecastle

foremast

cargo winch

windlass

masthouse

hatch coaming

bulwarks

no 2 hold

no 1 hold

stern

fore
peak
w.b.

forefoot

transverse bulkheads

Fig. 9 Comparative silhouettes of ocean-going merchant ships

a Cruise ship with accommodation for 840 passengers. *27,000 gt/210 m/M(2)/22k. Forward funnel removed in 1978 refit.

b Dutch general and refrigerated **cargo liner** on service between Europe and Gulf ports. 7,200 gt/162 m/M/17 k

c World's first triple screw **container ship** on service Japan to Europe via Panama Canal. 1972/53,500 gt/269 m/M/31 k 1842 containers—deck cargo not shown.

d British **crude oil tanker** 67,579 dwt/248 m/M/15·5 k

e British **products tanker** 15,922 dwt/169·40 m/M/14 k

f Japanese **container ship** for service between Japan and Pacific coast of North America—nearly 500 containers below deck and 212 above deck. 16,500 gt/186 m/22–26 k

g Dutch/German **LASH** vessel carries 83 loaded barges between USA and Europe. 1972/43,000 dwt/261·40 m/M/18 k

h Norwegian **car carrier** converted from British passenger liner 18,000 gt/176·80 m/M(2)/18 k. Purpose-built car carriers similar profile.

i Swedish **bulk lumber carrier** with deck cargo. British Columbia to Europe. 26,420 dwt/175·20 m/M15·5 k

j Canadian **bulk forest products carrier** British Columbia to UK, part-return cargo of phosphate rock from Florida to British Columbia. Equipped with three travelling Monck loaders. 21,461 gt/181 m/M14·5 k

---

* Building date/tonnage/overall length/method of propulsion and number of screws if more than one/service speed.

Passenger/cruise liner

As the name suggests, this type of ship is designed to carry a large number of passengers. Sizes and silhouettes do vary considerably, and with the recent trend in 'individual' funnels many ships can be identified quite easily by this feature alone. The

Fig. 10 MV* *Vistafjord* Br/1973/24,000 gt/ 190·82 m/M(2)20 k/650 passengers

By courtesy of Jim Prentice

profile of a passenger liner cannot be mistaken for any other type of ship. She has a high superstructure—often of four or more continuous decks—which occupies about three-quarters of the ship's overall length. On each side is a row of five or six lifeboats and many rectangular windows and, below this, the hull is pierced by long rows of cabin portholes on main, A, B, C and D decks. Forward of the navigating bridge, and aft of the superstructure, are pairs of derricks, or deck cranes, required for handling stores and possibly a very small amount of cargo. Just a few passenger liners (and these mainly Russian) now operate a regular service on the North Atlantic. The Cunard *Queen Elizabeth 2* maintains the Southampton–Cherbourg–New York service for part of the year with periods of cruising. The liner *France*, now *Norway*, and many other ships have

---

* In the captions, MV stands for motor vessel.

been sold or converted for cruising. New ships are now being built solely for cruising. From the observer's point of view there is no difference between the passenger liner on regular service and the cruising liner. Some of the custom-built cruise liners of the seventies, such as the ex-Cunarder *Sunward 2* and the *Song of Norway*, have deep clipper bows and a yacht-like appearance with emphasis on individual and often bizarre features such as the latter ship's funnel observation lounge. **Fig. 10** illustrates a liner with a traditional and very well-proportioned profile.

Fig. 11   The French trans-atlantic liner SS *France* which has now been converted as a Norwegian owned cruise ship—SS *Norway*

Fig. 12   TES *Canberra* Br/1961/43,975 gt/ 249·58 m/
TE(2)/27·5 k   *By courtesy of P & O*

Fig. 13 Comparative profiles of passenger/cruise liners of recent years

a

b

c

d

e

f

g

h

a *Norway* (ex-*France*) 1961 (refitted 1980)/70,000 gt/ 315 m/ST (2)/16–21 k/1,896 p* **(Fig. 11)**

b *Queen Elizabeth 2* Br/67,140 gt/294 m/DE (2) 28·5 k/1,815 p. North Atlantic service and world cruising. In 1982 fitted with 3 helipads and carried 3,500 troops to the Falklands at 25·5 knots **(Fig. 1)**.

c *Sea Princess* (ex-*Kungsholm*) Br/1966 (refitted 1979)/27,670 gt/210 m/M (2)/22 k/720 p

d *Europa* Ge/1981/34,500 gt/196 m/M (2)/22 k/600 p **(Fig. 16)**

e *Oceanic* Pa/1965/27,645 gt/238 m/ST (2)/26 k/ 1,035 p

f *Royal Viking Star* No/1971/28,221 205 m/M(2) 21 k/700 p. Lengthened 1983—two sisterships.

g *Sunward 2* No/1971/14,155 gt/148 m/M (2)/21 k/ 674 p. One class liner for short range cruises in semitropical waters.

h *Song of Norway* No/1969/25,000 gt/194 m/M (2)/ 21 k/1040 p. Designed for Caribbean luxury cruising. Deep clipper bow; can be distinguished by observation lounge on unusual funnel structure.

Fig. 14 Stern view of cruise liner *Aleksandr Pushkin* (USSR). Gross tonnage of nearly 20,000, length 176 m, and carries 600 passengers.

* p refers to approximate number of passengers.

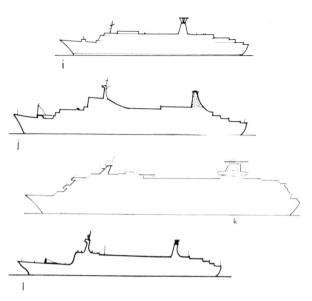

Fig. 15 Comparative profiles of passenger/cruise liners (2)

i *Maksim Gorkiy* (ex-*Hanseatic*) USSR/1968/29,981 gt/195 m/ST (2)/23 k/600 p. Easily distinguished by unusual funnel top.

j *Canberra* Br/1961/43,975 gt/249 m/TE (2)/27·5 k/ 1,706 p. Engines aft and two slender funnels. In 1982 fitted with two helipads and carried 2,000 troops to the Falklands (**Fig. 12**). Refit 1986.

k *Sovereign of the Seas* No/1988/74,000 gt/266 m/M/ 21 k/2276 p. The largest purpose-built cruise liner.

l *Eugenio C* It/1966/30,567 gt/217 m/ST (2)/27 k/ 1,400 p. With twin funnels aft, this ship bears some resemblance to *Canberra* and *Rotterdam*.

Some purpose-built cruise liners of the 1980s

Fyodor Dostoyevskiy USSR/1987/20,070 gt/176 m/ 20 k/656 p
Atlantic Lib/1982/20,000 gt/204 m/23 k/1292 p
Fairsky Lib/1984/22,000 gt/216 m/22 k/1776 p/ST
Nieuw Amsterdam Ne/1983/34,000 gt/214 m/21 k/ 1374 p
Royal Princess Br/1984/44,000 gt/232 m/22 k/1260 p
Song of America No/1982/37,000 gt/214 m/20 k/ 1575 p
Tropicale Li/1981/23,000 gt/204 m/19·5 k/1472 p
Holiday Pa/1985/46,000 gt/221 m/21·75 k/1800 p
Homeric Pa/1986/42,000 gt/204 m/23 k/1132 p
In service in 1988: *Seaward, Crown Odyssey, Royal Viking Excelsior, Star Princess, Jubilee, Fuji Maru* and others

By courtesy of Jim Prentice

Fig. 16 Cruise liner *Europa* (page 25)

Passenger/cargo liner

This once common type of intermediate liner has almost disappeared but there are signs of renewed interest. A new vessel for the UK-St Helena service will carry 125 passengers and 1,500 tonnes of cargo, and a 1988 Norwegian container ship, for South American services, will carry 64 passengers. A few UK, US and Polish freighters still carry up to 12 passengers.

a

b

c

d

e

Fig. 17 Variations of the cargo liner

General cargo liner

The ocean-going dry cargo liner, with a gross tonnage of between 5,000 and 12,000 gross tons, is designed for the transport of cargoes of many different types, shapes and sizes. The term *liner* is given to a vessel which operates on a regular service between ports, whereas the term *tramp* is given to a ship employed on charter to take cargo from port to port at any time, anywhere in the world. The cargo liner—referred to as a *freighter* in some countries—has four or five holds, and one or two tween decks which run for practically the full length of the ship, so that the varied items of cargo can be methodically stowed for convenient access at the relevant ports of discharge, and the weight of the cargo can more easily be distributed. These varied silhouettes are now being replaced by the more austere, mastless silhouette of the universal 'box' vessel as in Fig. 113. Until recently

---

a 6,000 gt ship with machinery amidships and five holds served by sixteen single derricks and a heavy lift jumbo derrick.

b 11,000 gt, 18 knot ship with engines three-quarter aft with holds served by sixteen derricks and three jumbos. Bipod masts and single kingposts. Bulbous bow (Fig. 6).

c Mastless cargo liner of 10,000 gt with machinery aft and six deck cranes.

d SD14 type general cargo vessel, 1967 onwards/14,000 dwt/141 m/M/14 k (see p 31).

e General and refrigerated cargo liner distinguished by patent Hallen 30-tonne derricks which are developed from the simple derrick so that all slewing and topping actions can be operated by one man at each derrick.

the cargo liner usually had machinery amidships, with an even placing of the holds fore and aft, but the recent trend is for the propelling machinery, and bridge superstructure to be either right aft or three-quarter aft.

Increased cargo space is made available in the shelter deck type of vessel. In the *closed shelter deck* (CSD) vessel the transverse bulkheads are carried right up to the shelter deck; in the *open shelter deck* (OSD) they are carried only as far as the main deck. In the latter type a small 1·21-m square opening is cut in the shelter deck and arranged so that it cannot be permanently closed.* Recent changes in tonnage assessment mean that a shelter deck vessel may have an alternative tonnage mark painted on the hull (see **Fig. 4**) so that the registered tonnage is assessed—open or closed—according to which tonnage mark is submerged.

The cargo-handling gear is obviously an important distinguishing feature of the cargo liner. It is arranged so as to ensure the minimum delay in loading or discharging cargo from all the holds and, if necessary, over both sides of the ship at the same time. Many ships now have deck cranes, or a mixture of cranes and derricks, patent Stülcken (**Fig. 21**) or Hallen derricks or Monck loaders (**Fig. 9j**). The simple mast, stayed by wire shrouds, is fast disappearing as strongly built self-supporting single and bipod masts take its place, with considerable reduction in maintenance costs and less obstruction during working operations.

During the Second World War nearly 3,000 standard 'Liberty' type general cargo ships were built with speed and economy. Twenty years later about

---

* Under these conditions the space between the main and shelter decks is not included in the tonnage on which harbour dues are calculated.

700 of them were still trading with a large number also in reserve. In 1967 the so-called SD14 (a shelter deck vessel of about 14,000 dwt) was designed as a Liberty ship replacement and within ten years about 150 of these standard vessels had been built, mainly at the Sunderland yards of Austin & Pickersgill, but also at other British yards and in Greece, Brazil and Argentina, under licence (**Fig. 17d** and **Fig. 18**).

Between 1970 and 1981 31 motor ships were built on the Clyde to the Cardiff class design bulk carrier. They were conceived as versatile ships capable of carrying, ore, grain, coal or forest products, and have large holds and unusually wide hatch openings. They are equipped with 4 or 5 electro-hydraulic cranes similar in appearance to those on **Fig. 17c**. The ship's profile shows a short compact bridge superstructure aft, a short forecastle and a bulbous bow. With a gross tonnage of 16,700 tonnes, an overall length of 175 m, the speed is 15·25 knots.

Fig. 18   Lamport & Holt ship *Belloc* built in 1979 to standard SD14 design

By courtesy of Jim Prentice

two 550—tonne cranes

ro–ro stern ramp

Fig. 19 *Happy Buccaneer* Ne/1984/16,341 gt

For some years now a number of general cargo liners have been fitted with heavy lift Stülcken derricks capable of lifting up to 180 tonnes (**Fig. 21**). Recently two types of heavy lift vessel have evolved. From the floating harbour crane has developed the self-propelled ocean-going ship (**Fig. 19**).

The *Happy Buccaneer* has two cranes each capable of lifting 550 tonnes which can work together to lift twice that weight. A module weighing up to 2,500 tonnes can be taken on board on the stern ramp. The other type is the semi-submersible heavy-lift vessel

Fig. 20 Norwegian *Ferncarrier* 1975/39,093 gt/225 m/M/16 k with Statoil drilling rig.
Foto Flite Ashford, Kent

evolved from the floating dock. She can submerge sufficiently for a cargo—a barge, vessel (page 158) or a drilling rig—to be floated on board and then rise again to her normal freeboard (**Fig. 112**). The *Ferncarrier* (**Fig. 20**) is the largest of this type; in 1983 she created a record when she carried a semi-submersible drilling rig from the builders in South Korea to the North Sea at an average speed of 13 knots over the 11,200 mile voyage.

By courtesy of Jim Prentice

Fig. 21   Kuwait motorship *Danah*, 15,446 gt, 1978

Fig. 22   A 9,000 ton vessel of the early 1960s

33

Fig. 23 1970s container ship of 15,000 gt and length of 212 m—speed 24 k

Container ship

During recent years an important development has taken place in the handling and transport of rail, road and seaborne freight with the introduction of the container, or unit/system. Traditional systems have involved numerous crates of miscellaneous shapes and sizes handled by different types of ships or quayside cranes. A completely integrated system has now emerged based on the use of standard ISO (International Standards Organization) box units of agreed dimensions: 2·44 m high and wide; and 6·06, 9·12 and 12·19 m long. The 6- and 12-m containers are those in general use. The majority of containers are designed for general dry cargo, but specialized units can take liquid, powder or refrigerated cargoes. Specially designed road vehicles, railway wagons, ships and dockside equipment handle these units in a co-ordinated way with speed and efficiency, and a minimum of manpower, providing a door-to-door service.

The container ship has a high freeboard and the superstructure is either right aft, or as in the drawing, three-quarter aft. The deck, with neither sheer nor camber, is unobstructed so that containers can be stacked on it in addition to those stowed below in the cellular holds. Handling of containers is by dockside transporter cranes and truck lifts, so that the vessel herself has only one or two small derricks for handling stores. Some of the container ships have stern, side or quantum doors so that road vehicles can drive aboard with their loads.

Ocean-going container ships are very expensive to build; therefore the general policy is for them to be owned, and operated, by a consortium of shipping companies (sometimes of different nationalities) with common interests on a particular route. For instance the Atlantic Container Line is formed of French, British, Dutch, German and Swedish interests, and Overseas Containers Ltd is composed of several British companies running a weekly service from the UK to Australia. (**Fig. 114**)

Fig. 24   An ocean-going container ship of 12,000 gt lying at a terminal, equipped with 25-tonne transporter cranes

Fig. 25   SS *Encounter Bay* Br/1969 converted from steam turbines to motorship in 1984.

By courtesy of P & O

Refrigerated ship or reefer

The traditional refrigerated fruit carrier is an elegant-looking, medium-sized, but fast, cargo liner. Usually painted white, she has no particular characteristics to distinguish her from the general cargo liner, although some vessels do have a long forecastle or a combined bridgedeck and forecastle. The fruit is carried in compartments insulated with cork, glass wool or other material, and kept at a temperature between $-30°$ C and $12°$C, according to the requirements of the fruit, each type needing a different temperature to keep it in good condition during the voyage.

Fig. 26 *English Star* Br/1985/9900 gt/151 m/M/20 k

Reefers in the fast fruit trade between South Africa and Europe are equipped to carry a wide range of fruits such as citrus fruits and deciduous apples and pears, whereas the ships on the West Indies to Europe trade usually specialize in carrying bananas. The *Geestbay* (**Fig. 27**) is owned by a combined British and Dutch company, carrying bananas to the ripening and distribution centre at Barry. Other well-known companies with reefers are Lauritzen (Denmark), Sven Salen (Sweden) and Fyffes of Britain.

The refrigerated meat carrier (**Fig. 26**) similarly has no particular outward feature for identification.

The Blue Star reefer (**Fig. 26**) is an excellent modern example of this class of ship. She is equipped to carry meat, dairy produce, fish, bananas, deciduous and citrus fruits in world-wide refrigerator trading. One feature, becoming usual, is that each crew member has a single cabin with private bath and toilet facilities. Another shipping company which has long had importance in the refrigerator trade is Lauritzen of Denmark; and in the UK the United Fruit Company, with its section of Fyffes, is well known in the banana trade. The all-embracing P & O also has a group of reefers absorbed from another company, and Hamburg South America takes an important part in the trade, too.

By courtesy of Geest Line

Fig. 27   Banana carrier MV *Geestbay*
Br/1981/8,000 gt/144 m/21 k/12 p

Specially designed refrigerated ship carries over 200,000 stems of bananas from the Windward Islands and Barbados to the UK, and British manufactured goods on the outward voyage. She has luxury accommodation for twelve passengers.

Short-sea trader

Generally well under 3,000 gross tons, the short-sea trader operates in the North Sea, Baltic, English Channel, Mediterranean, or in similar waters in any part of the world. She often runs, like the ocean-going liner, to a fixed schedule between ports.

Fig. 28 Short-sea trader of 1968

Modern vessels have machinery aft and a short, stocky superstructure. The short-sea trader may carry any type of cargo whether it is prepalletized, unit load, container or in the conventional mixed form. Well-equipped with cargo-handling gear, the ship can work in small ports where facilities are limited.

Fig. 29 A new style of short-sea trader with square funnel and transom stern. This vessel can carry 70 6-metre containers

The silhouette (**Fig. 28**) shows an example of the traditional short-sea cargo liner built to carry goods in many forms between the UK and Scandinavia, or the Mediterranean.

a   b

Fig. 30   Stern views of short-sea and ocean-going RO/RO vessels

The above photograph (a) shows some of the typical features of the newer style of short-sea trader. The hull is high and box-like to take the lorries and trailers which drive directly into the holds through the stern door set in the transom stern. This direct way into the holds requires that the motor exhausts are taken up the sides of the vessel through twin funnels. This particular feature has become essential in the RO/RO type of vessel. Photograph (a) shows a ship previously employed on the coastal service between Leith and Shetland. Photograph (b) shows the stern ramp of a Finnish RO/RO vessel of nearly 5,000 gt loading trailers at Gothenburg.

Fig. 31
Typical profile
of a 'Dutch'
coaster of just
under 500 gt

Coaster

No hard and fast rule can be drawn between the
coaster and the short-sea trader. No particular vessel
can, therefore, be identified primarily as a coaster, as
the small freighter between 300 and 1,500 gt may be
on charter (tramping), coasting or carrying cargo
on short-sea scheduled service. Many well-known
British coastal shipping companies no longer exist
owing to the development of heavy road transport.
Much of the remaining traffic is confined to bulk
cargoes of oil, coal, grain and fertilizers.

Fig. 32 British coaster, *Hoocreek* class, built in 1982
for coastal and short-sea trade; design based
on the estuarine motor barge. One new
feature is the engine control from the
bridge; length 49·99 m, with a tonnage of
1,235 gt. *FotoFlite, Ashford*

The West of Scotland steam puffer carried mainly
coal to the islands before the introduction of ro-ro

facilities. A 1942 steam puffer is preserved at the Scottish Maritime Museum at Irvine.

The so-called 'Dutch' coaster sailing under the flags of the Netherlands, Germany, Denmark, Norway and France has now become a very familiar sight in almost every British and Continental port. The strongly-built hull allows the vessel to lie on the ground at low tide, and the squat funnel and superstructure, and hinged mast, set in a tabernacle, enables her to negotiate low bridges. Most of these coasters have a gross tonnage of just under 500, because of certain regulations about the number of crew and watch-keeping duties; as a result of these regulations they are often referred to as 'paragraph' ships. With an average speed of 10 knots, comparatively powerful electric cargo-handling gear, and the features outlined above, the Dutch coaster is a handy vessel for service to upriver ports. Some coasters have their masts, placed against the forecastle and the bridge so that the well deck is clear for the stowage of a deck cargo of timber.

Fig. 33 Scottish motor puffer

Fig. 34 A 'Dutch' coaster of 300 gt built in 1971 and registered in Denmark

Oil Tanker (VLCC)

The first British tanker to exceed 100,000 tonnes deadweight was the *British Admiral*. Entering service in 1965 during a period of development in the transport of oil, she was broken up in 1976. The increasing demand for oil products, and other economic factors, led to the inception of the giant tanker to carry crude oil from the oilfields in Central America, or the Persian Gulf, to the centres of population such as north-west Europe. Much less costly to operate than a number of smaller vessels, the 300-metre tanker soon became a common feature of world shipping.

The VLCC (very large crude carrier) is easily

bulbous bow

Fig. 35   Typical profile of a 200,000 dwt VLCC, with a length of 325 m, i.e. longer than the *QE2* and *Norway*

Fig. 36   An 111,000 dwt tanker arriving at the BP terminal at Angle Bay, Pembrokeshire, with the motor tug *Thorngarth* in the foreground

By courtesy of BP

Fig. 37
The same VLCC with the manifold connected up to the shore installation. Deck cranes replace the normal hose-handling derrick

By courtesy of BP

distinguished by her immense size and very simple outline with a single bridge structure close to the stern. Many of the ships have a bulbous bow, but when the ship is down to her marks, it cannot be seen.

Many of these 1970s tankers are single-screw vessels propelled by steam turbines. With her very deep draught, the giant tanker's activities are limited to a few terminal ports; two methods of discharging the oil have been developed to offset this disadvantage. One method is to offload the cargo into smaller tankers in a deep, but sheltered, anchorage somewhere near the refineries, and the other is to discharge at a deepwater terminal and pump the oil overland to the refineries. Finnart, on Loch Long in the West of Scotland, is a terminal of the latter kind.

Fig. 38   A fully-laden tanker off Spithead on the way to the oil refineries at Fawley

Products tanker

The specialized carrier of oil in bulk now represents about one-third of the world total shipping tonnage. The products tanker is designed to transport either *clean* oil, i.e. motor spirit or kerosene, or *black* oil such as fuel and diesel oil, from refineries to discharge ports from whence it is distributed by road, rail, pipeline or sea. The giant crude oil tanker is a new development, but the conventional tanker has also increased in average size and is changing in appearance. In silhouette it retains the long, low outline, but the traditional three-island shape (**Fig. 40**) is giving way to the all-aft construction with the funnel, or twin funnels, bridge and accommodation all forming a single block on the poop (**Fig. 41**). In either form the islands are connected by a raised fore-and-aft gangway, or catwalk, which enables members of the crew to move from one island to another with safety in rough weather. This catwalk helps to identify the tanker and distinguish it from other bulk carriers. Additional characteristics are the numerous small tank hatches, fore-and-aft pipes and, amidships, the manifold with its complex arrangement of pipes and valves connected to the ship's tank system.

Fig. 39   The after end of an oil tanker

44

Fig. 40 A three-island type products tanker of 15,000 dwt built in 1962

The manifold is the focal point of the loading operations—by gravity or shore pumps—and discharging, by means of the ship's own pumps. Close to it are two light hose-handling derricks. The tanker hull is divided by two longitudinal and many transverse bulkheads forming up to thirty or so centre and wing cargo tanks. This number of comparatively small compartments minimizes the swishing effect of the liquid cargo and also means that several grades of oil can be carried on one voyage. At both ends of the cargo space there are double watertight bulkheads, known as cofferdams, to reduce the risk of fire spreading to the highly inflammable cargo. As the tanker transports her cargo on only one way of a round voyage, her crew spend the 'in ballast' run cleaning the tanks and preparing for the next cargo.

Fig. 41 'All-aft' tanker of 25,000 dwt built in 1973
By courtesy of Jim Prentice

Fig. 42
A British coastal
tanker of 1,570
tonnes dwt

Coastal spirit tanker

The coastal spirit tanker is a smaller version of the
ocean-going tanker. Her trips are usually short and
she may be employed on the same route between two
ports for many months, or even years. Obviously her
loading port is one of the oil refineries where the
spirit is produced; most ports have storage tanks into
which her cargo is discharged, preparatory to further
distribution. The coastal tanker has two islands—a
short forecastle and a poop with a single bridge
superstructure—which may be joined by a raised
section of the hull known as a trunk. The lower level
deck on each side of the trunk deck is only a few
centimetres above the water-line when the vessel is
loaded. As the tank tops are thoroughly watertight,
this very small freeboard presents no dangers.

Fig. 43
MV *Blackrock*
Br/1989/2,675 dwt/
78 m/10·3 k

FotoFlite, Ashford

One of a pair of British coastal tankers with a trunk
deck, raised forecastle and sunken poop. She is
designed to carry petrol, gas oil, kerosene and animal
and vegetable oils.

LPG **carrier**

The liquefied gas carrier is distinguished from the normal oil tanker, or bulk carrier, by the elaborate deck fittings and pipe work, and the horizontal pressure cylinders. On some ships there is a series of large conical or domed tank tops visible above deck level. This type of vessel is specially designed for the carriage of: propane, butane and natural gas methane.

|⟝———— trunk deck and pressure tanks ————⟞|

Fig. 44 An ocean-going LPG carrier of 15,000 dwt

Liquefied methane is carried in insulated tanks at a very low pressure and is cooled to its boiling-point. The mast amidships contains the vents from each tank. Like the oil tanker and bulk carrier, the ship has a number of wing and hopper tanks for water ballast.

Fig. 45 MV *Melrose* Br/1971/1,998 gt/86·95 m/ 13·5 k. A fully/semi-refrigerated Ethylene/ LPG tanker

By courtesy of Geo. Gibson & Co. Ltd

Bulk carrier

At first glance the bulk carrier may be mistaken for an oil tanker, as the long low silhouette and compact bridge superstructure are very similar, but on closer examination it will be seen that the bulk carrier lacks the catwalk and deck details of the tanker. The majority of bulk carriers have no derricks except a pair on the forecastle, or poop, for handling ship's stores. The loading and discharging of bulk cargoes—of grain, ore, cement, sugar, bauxite, industrial salt, phosphates or coal—is done by dockside cranes and grabs, and for this reason hatchways are wide and clear of obstructions. The silhouette line between the forecastle and the bridge may be broken by small projections which are either hold ventilators or part of the hatch control gear. The hatch covers are usually of the steel watertight patent type which are pulled clear of the hatches either by electric or hydraulic machinery. Some ore carriers do, however, have cargo-handling gear to enable the discharge of cargo into barges alongside (**Fig. 46**).

Fig. 46   A 35,000 dwt bulk carrier built in 1976 equipped with a series of deck cranes

Many vessels are designed to carry alternative cargoes; some have the dual purpose of carrying large numbers of cars on the outward run and iron ore on the return voyage. A new category of the 1980s is the 'combo' or multi-purpose bulk/container vessel capable of carrying general cargo, containers, liquids and vehicles—a development of the OBO.

Fig. 47 A typical 15,000 ton bulk carrier with no cargo-handling gear seen here discharging her cargo of grain by means of dockside suction grain elevators.

Fig. 48 The deck arrangement of an ore carrier showing the wide hatches, with a swimming-pool for the crew between Nos 5 and 6. The short mast forward has an enclosed 'crow's nest'. (**Fig. 114**) The largest dry bulk carrier is now a Norwegian vessel of 365,000 tonnes dwt.

Fig. 49 A 250 m OBO capable of carrying over 100,000 tonnes of cargo at a speed of 15 knots

OBO **carrier**

The dual, or multi-purpose, bulk carrier has developed in order to eliminate the necessity of making long return voyages in ballast. The oil/bulk/ore ship's hull is subdivided so that the holds for the bulk cargo, such as grain or ore, are flanked by oil tanks. There are also oil tanks between the floors of the holds and the ship's bottom. The OBO can be distinguished from the normal bulk carrier by the more elaborate hybrid deck fittings, with oil tank vents and piping—and a manifold—as well as the wide steel hatch covers. At a distance the additional feature of the central hose derricks can be picked out. As the 100,000 tonne deadweight OBO s are very costly vessels they are, like so many of the container ships, owned by a consortium of companies.

Fig. 50 An ex-Swedish OBO of 42,000 gt now owned in Greece

Skyfotos, Ashford, Kent

Car carrier

Fig. 51 A *Nosac* class car carrier with a tonnage of 12,000 gt and a speed of 20 knots **(Fig. 116)**

Mention has already been made of the bulk/car dual-purpose ship. Early in 1971 a new silhouette appeared on the shipping scene with the introduction of the Norwegian car carrier converted from the Royal Mail Line passenger cargo liner formerly on the UK–South America service. The new type had an unusually long and very high superstructure resembling the contemporary passenger/car ferry in outline but with no openings in the high topsides. Some vessels carry over 4,000 cars.

Following this, and other conversions the purpose-built car carrier appeared with similar characteristics. The drawing **(Fig. 51)** shows one of the *Nosac* class of car carriers belonging to Norwegian owners. With their prominent deck cranes, insignificant bridge superstructure and small funnel they are like no other merchant ship type. These particular ships have orange-coloured hulls.

An earlier 15,000-ton motor ship was designed as a dual-purpose vehicle bulk ship with holds equipped with hoistable false decks capable of carrying 1,750 Volkswagen vehicles on the outward passage from Hamburg. On her return voyage, often through the St Lawrence Seaway, she carried either grain, or ore, in bulk.

The purpose-built car carriers are sometimes known as PCTC's, i.e. Pure Car and Truck Carriers.

Barge carriers

In the early 1970s an entirely new conception of sea transport came into being with the introduction of the Lighter Aboard Ship (LASH) system. Vessels of this type are large, low ships with no sheer and very little superstructure. A huge gantry crane, with a lifting capacity of about 500 tonnes, is used to lift the laden lighters 18·75 m long and 9·5 m wide, from water level (at the stern) to be stowed either in one of the five holds or on deck. The ship can carry a total of 83 fully laden lighters—49 in the holds and 34 on deck. In port they are lifted from the stowed position, lowered to water level and towed away without the use of quay space.

Fig. 52   LASH ship MV *Rhine Forest* (ex *Bilderdyk*) Lib/1972/44,000 dwt/261 m/18 k

The first LASH route was between New Orleans and Rotterdam and Sheerness—all three ports serving as centres of inland and intracoastal waterways linking large areas of industry and population. A ship is shown in **Fig. 52**. The service provides a door-to-door transport method far into the interior of Europe or North America without need for quayside delays and handling. Similar services are operated by BACAT (Barge Aboard CATamaran) and Seabees (Lykes Lines) vessels. The latest BACO and CONDOCK vessels carry both barges and containers (**Fig. 118**).

Fig. 53
Aberthaw Fisher
Br/1966/2,355 gt/
83·52 m/
DE(2)/11 k

two 50-tonne derricks
twin funnels stowed position
adjustable link span
vehicle deck
hydraulic lift to hold

Heavy lift coaster

This unusual looking vessel is one of two specialized carriers built for James Fisher & Sons Ltd for the transport of very heavy, and difficult, items of machinery. For this purpose, one of them is on long-term charter to the Central Electricity Board for the transport of transformers and other bulky items required for the construction of power stations. The distinctive feature is the large central goal post with its two 50-tonne derricks which are stowed in the vertical position when the ship is at sea. The cargo, whether a transformer or a diesel locomotive, is winched across the link span at the stern on to the vehicle deck. At the forward end of this deck it is transferred to the hydraulic lift and then lowered into the hold. The link span at the stern can be raised or lowered to correspond with the level of the quay. As the superstructure is so far forward, and the long clear deck is an obvious feature, the heavy lift coaster may be mistaken for an oil rig supply vessel (page 69) or perhaps, at a distance, for a salvage tug.

Fig. 54 Looking forward along the vehicle deck of the *Aberthaw Fisher*

a | funnel | hinged masts | bridge

flatiron

b

all aft

c

raised quarter deck

Fig. 55 Three types of collier

Collier

The collier is a medium-sized bulk carrier which is normally operated on coastal and short-sea routes. Usually a single deck vessel, i.e. with no tween decks, it has three to five holds, very large hatches and high hatch coamings. No cranes or derricks are fitted, as the collier loads her cargo at gravity tips and discharges it at special wharves equipped with quayside grab cranes; the extra wide hatches give the grabs greater access to all parts of the holds. Sometimes the holds are U-shaped in section so that the cargo will tend to level out by gravity and trim itself; in this case the collier is referred to as 'self-trimming'.

Owing to the increase in the use of North Sea gas, and the development of oil-fired and nuclear power stations in Great Britain, the number of coastal colliers has been drastically reduced. Most of the Thames upriver colliers, known as *flatirons* (**Fig. 55**), so familiar to Londoners as they negotiated the bridges with lowered masts, have been sold and a few have gone into the grain trade. These *flatirons*, had a very low bridge, a hardly discernible funnel, and short masts which could be lowered on a hinged tabernacle. The drawing **Fig. 55b** shows a flush-decked collier with raised forecastle and machinery aft employed in carrying 7,000 tonnes of coal from the Humber and north-east ports to London and the south of England, at an average speed of twelve knots. The lower drawing **c** is a raised three-quarter deck motor collier, with an island bridge, a once familiar type which is rapidly disappearing.

By courtesy of Cory Maritime Ltd

Fig. 56   MV *Cora*—a 12 knot ex-British collier now owned in Italy; 1965/4,840 gt/112·80 m/12 k

A collier with the typical wide hatches and lack of derricks or deck cranes. This single deck ship, with four self-trimming holds, carries over 7,000 tonnes of small particle coal to power stations where it is discharged by quayside grabs.

RO/RO passenger/car ferry

The traditional cross-channel packet was a fast steam turbine vessel resembling a miniature passenger liner. With the widespread and continual growth of road transport, and the private car, this elegant type of ship has been almost entirely superseded by the much heavier-looking motor vessel with a high freeboard, three- or four-deck superstructure, and twin funnels placed athwartships. This latter arrangement allows unobstructed vehicle decks, although some of the ferries do retain the central funnel, and many of the twin funnel vessels even have a large central dummy funnel as well. These new ships are designed with facilities for quick loading and discharging so that car drivers themselves can drive on and off over hydraulically operated bow and/or stern ramps. In port the bow ramp, or vizor, can easily be recognized in its raised position, but at sea it forms an unobtrusive watertight closure. Not all the ferries have this bow ramp; some have side doors instead, in addition to the universal stern door and ramp.

Passenger/car ferries vary considerably in size. The two 15,000 gt ferries on the UK/Sweden run, and even the *Finlandia* **(Fig. 117)**, are exceeded by

Fig. 57 Internal deck arrangement of a RO/RO passenger/car ferry on the North Sea

stern door and ramp

bow door and ramp

main vehicle deck

engine room

car decks   car decks

56

By courtesy of Jim Prentice

Fig. 58 British built passenger and car ferry *Norsea* on trials on the Firth of Clyde, March 1987

the two 31,727 gt passenger ferries *Norsea* and *Norsun* on the Hull-Rotterdam route, jointly owned by P & O and Nedlloyd. With a length of 179 metres they can accommodate 1,250 passengers and, with access by the single stern door, 850 cars on three vehicle decks. Another giant ferry is the 30,000 gt *Koningin Beatrix* on the Harwich-Hook of Holland route.

Within the British Isles there are many passenger/car ferries not only across to the Continent and Ireland, but also in the Clyde estuary, from the mainland of Scotland to the Western Isles, Orkney and Shetland. With so many ferries in these and similar waters, used by thousands of holidaymakers, this type of ship is now very familiar.

RO/RO unit load ship

Fig. 59 shows the simple outline of a new vessel designed for the North Sea from the UK to Sweden. The ship can carry 123 twelve-metre trailers or 462 TEU's, i.e. that number of 6·06 m containers. The stern door and ramp are operated hydraulically with lifts to the upper deck. Propulsion is by two

Fig. 59   Typical RO/RO unit load ship

controllable pitch propellers and a bow thrust unit is fitted forward. If conventionally packed, or crated, cargo is delivered at the quayside and can be packed in containers before shipment. Some units are conveyed on road transport vehicles and therefore accommodation is provided for twelve lorry drivers.

This particular twin-screw vessel has no cargo-handling gear as this is unnecessary for the type of cargo she carries. Similar ships equipped as multi-purpose vessels do have derricks or deck cranes.

Fig. 60   The *Dana Maxima* Da/1978/6552
dwt/141 m/18 k

By courtesy of Danish Seaways

The RO/RO vessel shown above operates between the UK and Denmark carrying containers as well as trailers. She has a single funnel on the port side and a prominent 10-tonne travelling gantry for moving containers.

Fig. 61 Swedish Train Ferry *Trelleborg*

The world's largest train ferry runs on the 4-hour crossing between the Swedish port of Trelleborg and Sassnitz in East Germany. Built in 1982, this 10,882 gt ship accommodates either 50 railway wagons or a mixture of 10 passenger coaches and a number of wagons; 130 cars can be carried, plus 800 passengers (page 60).

Fig. 62 MV *Horsa* Br/1972/5,590 gt/117·30 m /19·5 k/1,400 p/210 cars or 38 lorries
By courtesy of Sealink British Ferries

Fig. 63   *Nord pas de Calais*
Fr/1988/13,727 gt/160 m/22·5 k

FotoFlite, Ashford

Train ferry

In appearance, the train ferry does not differ very
much from the RO/RO passenger/car ferry. The
comparatively broad beam, high freeboard, lack of
derricks, stern port and lack of sheer are features
common to both types. Exceptions are some of the
large train ferries running across the southern Baltic,
which are much more like versions of passenger
liners. The essential part of the train ferry is the long
continuous main deck, which may be fitted with four
tracks, giving a total of up to 360 metres of rails.
Access to this rail deck is through a stern, or bow
port over a link span connecting the ship's rails to the
terminal rail tracks.

Ferries carrying passengers are equipped with
dining saloons and other public rooms, and therefore
have many more portholes, side windows and
lifeboats, and greater promenade space than the
freight train only ferry. Drawing **Fig. 64** shows a
modern ship on the 4-hour crossing between Trelleborg in Sweden and the East German port of Sassnitz

(**Fig. 61**). Other ferries ply between Denmark and Germany, e.g. MV *Danmark* (1968/6,300 gt) with accommodation for twelve railway coaches, wagons, road vehicles, and 1,500 passengers.

The train ferry (**Fig. 63**) carries 45 wagons, articulated wagons and 80 passengers between Dover and Dunkerque.

Other, mainly, freight only, train ferries with similar characteristic features, include those which operate between: Denmark and Sweden, Sweden and Finland, the mainland of Italy and Messina; there are also six inter-island services in Japan. In eastern Canada train ferries connect New Brunswick with Newfoundland and, south of the Great Lakes is a system of non-self-propelled freight wagon ferries between Detroit, Michigan and Windsor.

Fig. 64

MV *Trelleborg* Sw /1982/10,882 gt/170 m/M/19 k

Estuarial ferry

Passenger and car ferries operating in comparatively sheltered waters vary a good deal in size and in general appearance. Some of them resemble the RO/ RO short-sea ferries already illustrated, while others

61

are not much more than self-propelled double-ended pontoons. The time spent on passage can vary from a few minutes to perhaps one hour or more.

Fig. 65a   MV *Lord of the Isles* (1989) is a passenger/car ferry with stern and side loading ramps, operating off the west coast of Scotland

By courtesy of J. Aikman Smith

Fig. 65b   *Netley Castle* (1974) operating between Southampton and Cowes, on the Isle of Wight, in sheltered waters

In all parts of the world where thousands of daily commuters must cross from one city to an adjacent one, or from one part of a city to another, there are variations on the passenger ferry. The less sheltered the waters, and the longer the passage, the more the ferry will have a shiplike appearance.

Fig. 66 Hovercraft on English Channel route

The hovercraft is a raft-like vessel that rides on an enclosed cushion of air on either land or sea. Propulsion is by four variable-pitch air screws powered by gas turbines that also drive the centrifugal lift fans for the air cushion. A 40 m hovercraft (**Fig. 66**), with a beam of 23 m, can accommodate 424 passengers and 55 cars and make the crossing (or 'flight') from Dover to Calais, or Boulogne, in less than half the time taken by the fastest ferry. Similar services operate across the Straits of Gibraltar, in Hong Kong and several South American routes.

Fig. 67 Hydrofoil

Generally smaller than the hovercraft, this type of vessel works on quite a different principle. The true boat-shaped hull is fitted with projecting planes or foils so that, at speed, the hull rises above the water and skims on the surface on the foils. **Fig. 67** shows a hydrofoil with 120 passengers but no cars. The jetfoil looks similar but is powered by water jets.

Fig. 68
PS *Waverley*
Br/1947/
693 gt/
75·63 m/
SR/14 k
*By courtesy of
Jim Prentice*

Paddle steamer

After a history of more than a century and a half the paddle steamer has now become a museum piece. In her later days she was represented only by two categories of vessel—tugs and excursion vessels operating in sheltered waters. The side paddles enabled the ship to make quick turns and rapid manoeuvres alongside piers, particularly in strong currents. This great advantage is now obtained by the use of Voith–Schneider propellers and bow thruster units (page 17). The excursion paddle steamer was always distinctive with her slender funnels, sharply raked masts. light superstructure and semi-circular paddle boxes, often decorated in colour and gold leaf. Many of the steamers were able to accommodate about two thousand passengers on day excursions.

The last seagoing paddle steamer is the *Waverley*, owned by the Paddle Steamer Preservation Society and used for summer excursions in the Clyde estuary and elsewhere round the UK. Caledonian Mac-Brayne ran the *Maid of the Loch* (1953) on Loch Lomond in summer until 1982. Only just in time, before the final disappearance of this attractive type of ship, groups of enthusiasts have made successful attempts to preserve a few of the survivors. Founded in 1959 the Paddle Steamer Preservation Society later acquired the last of the River Dart passenger paddle steamers, *Kingswear Castle* (1924), running her themselves during the summer. Some of the last paddle steamers have been preserved as floating restaurants or club houses. Some paddlers still operate on European rivers and on the Italian and Swiss lakes. In Norway the 1856 *Skibladner* runs during the summer on Lake Mjösa.

A few paddle tugs have been successfully saved from the ship breakers. The steam tug *Eppleton Hall* (1914) recently made a remarkable 10,000-mile, six-month voyage from England to San Francisco, to her museum resting-place alongside the restored Scottish sailing ship *Balclutha*. The *John H. Amos* (1931) is under renovation at Chatham, and the Maritime Trust purchased the *Reliant* (1907) for preservation in the National Maritime Museum at Greenwich.

Of the ex-Humber paddle ferries, *Lincoln Castle* and *Tattershall Castle* are floating restaurants in Grimsby and London respectively. *Wingfield Castle* is undergoing renovation at Hartlepool. As recently as the 1950s paddle tugs were built for the Royal Navy for work in the naval dockyards. They were diesel-electric vessels with twin funnels placed abreast. Of the many large, and very decorative, stern-wheel paddlers formerly running on the Mississippi, and other North American rivers, the *Delta Queen*, registered at Cincinnati, and the more modern *Mississippi Queen* are both employed on excursions of several days' length between New Orleans and Memphis. A new stern-wheeler of this type is now under construction for the same excursions.

Fig. 69 Tug *Tirrick* Br/ 1983/482 gt/37 m/12·5 k Service at Sullom Voe oil terminal in Shetland

By courtesy of Jim Prentice

Fig. 70 Motor Tug *Gannet* Br/ 1967/143 gt/ 1,200 hp

This harbour tug is propelled by two Voith-Schneider units. She has the towing hook close to the stern and lacks the usual towbeams.

Fig. 71 Motor Tug *Cathaigh* (ex-*Flying Falcon*) Eire/1968/ 213 gt/1,470 hp/12·5 k

Propelled by a Kort nozzle unit, this vessel is equipped for fire-fighting duties, particularly at oil installations.

* Horse-power (hp) to be replaced by kW metric units.

Fig. 72

Motor Tug *Flying Scout*
Br/1970/290
gt/2,800 hp/
14 k/Kn

twin exhausts

towing hook
and winch

radar

strongback
above winch

rubbing strake and tenders

Tug

Whatever her size, the tug can rarely be mistaken for
any other type of vessel. She has high bows, a short
superstructure set far forward, and the funnel (or
twin funnels) and mast close to the wheelhouse. The
fixed or spring-loaded towing hook is at the after end
of the superstructure and, so that the towline does
not foul the after-deck fittings, they are protected by
transverse, curved steel hoops known as towbeams
or strongbacks. Many of the newest motor tugs have
twin exhausts incorporated in the mast structure.
The tug's engines need to be very powerful and, to
increase her manoeuvrability, the controllable pitch
propeller and Kort nozzle are now commonly fitted;
some tugs have Voith–Schneider units instead of the
conventional propellers. Two-speed gear gives
greater accuracy of control at low speeds, particularly
against strong tides.

Every port has at least one tug equipped with fire-
fighting apparatus, which consists of foam and fire
monitors working from a platform on the mast.
American tugs—known as towboats—differ in appearance from the normal European vessel, as
regulations for crew accommodation result in a
longer superstructure. Moreover, these tugs usually
push and nose ships about harbours instead of towing
them. Many of the river tugs, generally handling a
string of barges, are built with a flat stem and
projecting 'buffers' for pushing.

Salvage tug

The ocean-going salvage tug is the largest of the family and she may be employed in towing a floating dock halfway round the world, or an oil rig from shipyard to drilling station. But most of her time is spent patrolling the international shipping lanes, just waiting for a distress signal. When this is received the tug, and others who have heard the signal, race to the disabled ship to compete for the salvage work. A Dutch company has long dominated this field, but

Fig. 73
Salvage Tug *Uragan*
USSR/1961/1,151
gt/61·00 m/17k

giant German tugs are now available. The most powerful British salvage tug in her time was the *Lloydsman* built in 1971 but now sold to a Singapore based company and renamed *Salviscount*. She is capable of towing the largest VLCC at 7 knots and has a speed of 18·5 knots when running free. Much of her efficiency and power comes from a controllable pitch propeller in a Towmaster 5·2-metre diameter Kort nozzle with aerofoil steering vanes (see **Fig. 5**). As well as a wide range of salvage equipment, which includes two 10-tonne derricks, this tug is equipped with foam and water fire monitors on the foremast.

Fig. 74
British salvage and anchor-handling tug *Salvageman*, built in 1980; 1,589 gt, length 69 metres. ORSV in background
FotoFlite, Ashford

Fig. 75 MV *Majestic Service*
Br/1971/692 gt/
56·22 m

Oil rig supply vessel (ORSV)

This new type can be seen in various ports associated
with underwater drilling for oil. She resembles a
large tug—in fact towing may be one of her tasks—
with the forward superstructure and clear working
deck aft. The main functions of the ship are to carry
stores, fuel oil, drilling water, cement, drilling gear
and personnel to the offshore rigs, and to tow the rigs
themselves to new stations and to handle their heavy

Fig. 76
MV *Smit-Lloyd
41* Ne/1971/
744 gt/52·70 m/
13 k

anchor gear. All this work may have to be done in
extremely bad weather and, therefore, the ships are
seaworthy and powerful. The cargo deck can be
manoeuvred under the rig platform for offloading
pipes, casing and other items. On some ships cylin-
drical cement tanks are fixed at the forward end of
the working deck, and others are fitted with a mobile
gantry crane which runs the full length of this deck.

69

Fig. 77   *Dan Baron*, ex-British drill ship now owned
in the Bahamas; 8,000 gt/136 m

Oil drilling vessel

With the rapid and extensive increase in the number
of underwater oilfields in various parts of the world,
some new types of ships have evolved. Many of the
huge drilling platforms bear no resemblance what-
soever to a ship (**Fig. 78**) but some purpose-built and
converted ships are in use. **Fig. 77** above shows a
vessel converted from a bulk carrier in 1976. The
Polly Bristol was purpose-built in 1980 with diesel-
electric propulsion and eight point mooring facilities.
The high drilling tower and helicopter platform are
distinctive features.

A drilling ship must have powerful anchoring
gear at the bows and stern to enable her to remain
stationary against the forces of heavy seas, strong
currents, long period swell and strong winds. Some
of the purpose-built ships have a large rectangular
well under the derrick through which the drill passes
to the sea-bed, while on other ships the drilling
operations are done outboard on a cantilevered
platform. Other features of the drilling vessel are
large racks for stowage of standard lengths of drill
pipe and oilfield casing, and a laboratory for the
study of drill cores. Non-visible features include
large tanks for carriage of liquid and bulk mud, bulk
cement, and oil. The British *Ben Ocean Lancer* (1977)
is one of the most advanced drilling vessels; she can
drill in water depths down to 900 m while remaining
in position without anchors.

Fig. 78   An ORSV of 480 gt built in 1968

The vessel lies close to a BP oil rig, in the Firth of Forth, where she has been towed for the renewal of the rig's anchor wires. This ORSV is owned by a consortium of P & O and French, Dutch and Norwegian interests. She can carry up to 700 tonnes of drilling gear and has accommodation for twelve passengers.

Fig. 79

Navigation buoys on the foredeck of a Northern Lighthouse Commission tender at Granton about to leave on a four-day servicing voyage

Lighthouse tender

The lighthouse tender is a small vessel with a long superstructure and generally has a smart and well cared for appearance. The two main functions are firstly, to service navigation buoys and secondly, to carry relief crews and supplies to lighthouses on island and rock stations, and lightships. The ship is equipped with a heavy derrick on the foremast, so that buoys can be lifted out of the water and placed on deck.

Fig. 80 Trinity House tender *Patricia* 1982/2,540 gt/86·5 m/DE/14 k (**Fig. 119**)

Navigation buoys and lights in England and Wales are under the general authority of Trinity House; those in Scotland and the Isle of Man are under the Commissioners of Northern Lights, and those in Ireland are under the Commissioners of Irish Lights. The flags of ships under these authorities are shown in **Fig. 110**. Some large estuaries, e.g. the Firth of Clyde, are under separate navigation authorities responsible for all buoys and navigation lights.

For well over a century and a half moored **light vessels** have been manned but increasingly they are being replaced by fully automatic vessels controlled and monitored from a land-based depot. A light vessel of 1933 is now preserved at Anstruther, Fife. Some have been replaced by Large Automatic Navigation Buoys (LANBYs) and others, un-manned, have been entirely automated.

Lifeboat

The service of the Royal National Lifeboat Institution (founded 1824) is unique as it is financed entirely by voluntary subscription. On the shores of Great Britain, Northern Ireland and Eire lifeboats are permanently on station, with a number of small inflatable boats, mainly at seaside resorts in the summer. The larger boats, like the *Clyde* and *Arun* (**Fig. 81**) are usually close to the busier shipping lanes, and to the more treacherous stretches of coast. Except at Humberside (Spurn Point), the crews are part-timers who are always ready to respond to emergency calls. Lifeboats must have powerful engines, good reserves of buoyancy, and be very manoeuvrable in heavy seas. RNLI boats have blue hulls and, for easier visibility at sea, orange upper works.

CLYDE 21·4m   D – Inflatable dinghy

ARUN 15·8 or16·5m

WAVENEY 13·4m

OAKLEY 11·3m

Fig. 81   Shore-based Lifeboat: four main types used by the *Royal National Lifeboat Institution*. The 14·3 m *Tyne* and 12 m *Mersey* classes have been added and the *Oakleys* are being phased out.

Cable ship

The earlier steam cable layers were very yacht-like in appearance, and even contemporary motor vessels have retained something of the same character. The deeply curved clipper stem, with sheaves and gantry, is the most obvious feature, and the long superstructure, many portholes, and several lifeboats all indicate a large complement of crew and cable engineers. Cable layers are generally within the range of 5/6,000 gross tons.

The function of this type of ship is either to lay new telephone cable (which is about 30 mm in diameter) or to inspect and repair existing cable. New cable is paid out over the stern sheaves from huge vertical tanks which can hold up to 3,000 kilometres of cable. Existing cable is grappled for over the bow sheaves, inspected, and repaired as required before it is returned to the sea-bed. The cable ship must be easily manoeuvrable so she is fitted with a bow thruster and, as in the case of the ship illustrated, with an activated rudder and controllable pitch propeller. **Fig. 82** shows the profile of two ships equipped for shallow and deep-water work in any part of the world from the Arctic to the Tropics. They incorporate a new system of pan loading in which the cables are loaded in very large containers—like giant cassettes. The 1922 *John W. Mackay* has been preserved in London's Museum of Dockland. The 1984 addition to the Cable & Wireless fleet is the diesel-electric *Pacific Venture*, designed to work on the new cable between Australia and New Zealand and Canada.

twin funnels
helicopter platform
bow gantry and sheaves
crane
active rudder
cable tanks
bow thruster

Fig. 82
British PO cable ship,
1973/3,500 disp/94·50 m/M

74

Fig. 83
DES *Perkun*
Po/1963/
1,152 gt/
56·38 m/
DE(2)/14 k

strengthened ice belt

towing winch

port and starboard heeling tanks

fore screw

stern screws

A, B & C = water ballast trimming tanks

Icebreaker

In Canada, Russia and the Baltic many ferries and
other craft have hulls which are strengthened for
navigation in ice, but harbour and seagoing ice-
breakers are specially constructed to clear passages
for others. The all-welded hull is different from any
other type of vessel. So that the cleared passage is
wide enough for the following ships, the icebreaker's
beam must be a metre or so wider than theirs and, to
give the maximum manoeuvrability her own length
must be comparatively short; therefore the beam-
length ratio is about 1:5. The drawing shows the
deeply-cut stem that enables the icebreaker to ride
up onto the ice and crush it by sheer weight, which
is increased when water ballast is pumped into the
forward trimming tanks. Side trimming tanks are
used to give a rocking or heeling motion. The hull
plating is strengthened at the water-line by a 6-metre
band with a thickness of between 30 and 50 milli-
metres. The rounded section of the ship's sides—
known as the tumblehome—helps to force her
upwards in reaction to the side pressure from the ice.
The Russian *Lenin*, built in 1959, is a huge triple-
screw icebreaker propelled by turbo-electric nuclear
power. She has a length of 134 metres to a beam of
27·63 metres; running free she can maintain a speed
of eighteen knots.

Fig. 84 *Mersey Venture* (1983)

Trailing suction dredger

The seagoing suction dredger is an engines aft vessel not unlike the coastal tanker in profile, but distinguishable by the much greater complexity of the gear between the forecastle and the navigating bridge. This gear consists of a horizontal suction, or drag pipe, suction pipe hoisting machinery and boom, and discharge gear for operating the hopper bottom doors. During dredging operations the suction pipe is trailed along the sea-bed and the spoil is pumped into the hopper. When this is full, the ship steams out to the dumping ground and the spoil is discharged by gravity, or it may be pumped ashore for land reclamation.

The *Mersey Venture* (2,647 gt) is a highly automated dredger with a capacity of 2,200 cubic metres and can dredge to a depth of 20 metres. Another form of suction dredger (**Fig. 85**) is used to dredge marketable sand and gravel for building and civil engineering purposes. It works like the harbour-deepening dredge, but the cargo is discharged ashore at special wharves.

Fig. 85
A sand and gravel suction dredger returning to port with her cargo

Fig. 86 MV *Gardyloo* Br/1976/2,000 gt/86 m
By courtesy of Jim Prentice

Sludge disposal vessel

The sludge vessel may be seen in most estuaries associated with large centres of population such as the Thames, Clyde or the Mersey. Full treatment of sewage results in large quantities of sludge, which is pumped from the sewage works to the disposal vessel's tanks. This is then conveyed out to sea to specific dumping grounds and discharged by gravity. **Fig. 86** shows the modern vessel that carries sludge from Leith (Edinburgh) down the Forth to dumping grounds off St Abb's Head or the Bell Rock. **Fig. 87** shows a vessel owned by the Strathclyde Regional Council. With the recent demand for pollution-free seas, more land sewage systems are being installed and sludge vessels will be phased out.

Fig. 87
MV *Dalmarnock*
Br/1970/2,050 gt/
95·11 m/11·5 k

The *Dalmarnock* might be mistaken for a coastal tanker but for the three large ventilators. On her daily voyage with 3,000 tonnes of sludge she takes about four hours to reach the dumping grounds.

Fig. 88   Dredging craft

Grab dredger and hopper

In its simplest form the grab dredger is a pontoon
with a slewing and hoisting crane capable of operating a double-chain grab. Many improvised craft are
like this, but others have a seaworthy hull and
propelling machinery. The grab dredger has an
advantage over the bucket dredger in docks and
basins, as it can work in awkward corners. The spoil
may be either transferred directly to a hopper
alongside or, if the craft is self-propelled, carried to
the dumping grounds out at sea, or, alternatively
discharged at a land reclamation unit. The upper
drawing **a** shows the outline of an old type single
crane grab dredger and **b** is a self-propelled self-
discharging motor hopper with a twin rudder-pro-
peller unit and a length of 63·63 metres. She has an
unusual arrangement of three funnel exhausts. The
dumb hopper (**c**), as the name implies, has no
propelling machinery and it is necessary for her to
be either towed, or pushed out to the spoil grounds
by a tug (**d**). Her spoil is discharged by gravity
through bottom-opening doors.

Bucket ladder dredger

The bucket ladder dredger has no hopper space, so the spoil must be transferred to hopper barges alongside. It may or may not be self-propelled. The hull has an open well through which the ladder can be lowered to a depth that may be down to 21 metres. The endless belt of buckets, each with a capacity of

Fig. 89 The working of a bucket dredger

0·5 to 0·7 m^3, moves round and, as each bucket reaches the bottom, it scoops up some spoil and carries it to the top of the ladder. A tripping device tips the bucket and empties the spoil into a chute down into the hopper barge.

Fig. 90 Twin-screw motor bucket ladder *Blythswood* Br/1963/786 gt/64·00 m working on the River Clyde

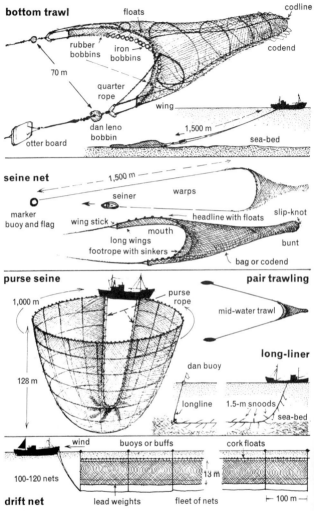

bottom trawl

floats
codline
rubber bobbins
iron bobbins
codend
70 m
quarter rope
wing
dan leno bobbin
1,500 m
otter board
sea-bed

seine net

1,500 m
seiner
warps
marker buoy and flag
wing stick
headline with floats
slip-knot
mouth
long wings
footrope with sinkers
bunt
bag or codend

purse seine

1,000 m
purse rope
128 m

pair trawling

mid-water trawl

long-liner

dan buoy
longline
1.5-m snoods
sea-bed

wind
buoys or buffs
cork floats
100-120 nets
13 m
100 m
drift net
lead weights
fleet of nets

Fig. 91 Methods of fishing

3 FISHING VESSELS

Methods of Fishing

Trawling The bottom trawl is a large conical bag of net which is dragged along the sea-bed to catch demersal fish such as cod, plaice and haddock. The mouth of the net is held open by the kite-like action of the two otter boards. The lighter mid-water floating trawl—without ground bobbins—is towed by one, or a pair of trawlers to catch non-bottom feeding, or pelagic, fish such as herring, mackerel and sprats. **Seining** The seine net is also conical but has neither ground bobbins nor otter boards. The two long warps, and the net, are paid out in the form of a triangle, and, when the boat returns to its marker buoy, the net is drawn in with its catch of flatfish, cod and haddock. **Purse seining**, similar to Scottish pair boat ring-netting, has grown rapidly in recent years with the development of large, light, nylon nets and the power block. The huge net is shot in an arc and the two ends gradually drawn together to enclose the shoal in the bag, or purse. The purse-rope is drawn in and the bag reduced in size until the catch is brought alongside in the bunt. This method is widely used for catching herring, pilchard, sardine, sardinella, anchoveta, mackerel and tuna. **Long-lining** is used to catch haddock, ling and cod where the sea-bed is rocky and uneven. The hundreds of hooks are baited with pieces of herring or mussel. **Drifting** The drift net consists of a meshed screen of gillnets several kilometres in length in which the herring and other pelagic fish are caught by their gills. This traditional, passive form of fishing—employed at night when the fish feed nearer the surface—is being replaced by less arduous active methods of purse-seining and mid-water trawling.

side trawler

fore gallows

fish tackle

after derrick

boat davit

gilson

yo-yo

whaleback forecastle   trawl winch   after gallows

Fig. 92   Deep-sea side trawler for middle-water fishing

Trawler

The trawler is engaged in all-the-year-round fishing, often in some of the stormiest waters in the world, and must therefore be a strong, sturdy vessel able to work in the worst of weather. The side trawler has a pronounced sheer, a superstructure placed well aft and a clear foredeck fitted with compartments, or fish pounds, for sorting the catch. During the towing operations the trawl-warps pass through pulleys in the fore, and aft, gallows. Some trawlers have these on the starboard side only and others on both sides. Another characteristic of the trawler is the powerful winch placed just forward of the wheelhouse. Present-day trawlers are well equipped with marine electronics, i.e. navigators, auto-pilots, radar and sonar equipment for fish locating. Three main categories of trawlers operate from British ports. *Distant-water* trawlers with lengths of 50/85 m fish,

Fig. 93   Middle-water side trawler

Fig. 93
The changed profile of the modern fishing vessel with prominent shelter-deck

high freeboard – full or part length shelter deck casing

mainly for cod, in the Barents Sea, off Greenland, Spitsbergen and Newfoundland, often making round voyages of up to 5,000 miles from the main ports of Hull, Grimsby and Fleetwood. *Middle-water trawlers*, with lengths of about 50 m, operate from Aberdeen and Fleetwood to the North Cape and the White Sea. *Near-water trawlers* based on Aberdeen and Lowestoft are 30/40 m vessels mainly fishing in the North Sea, while a large number of smaller vessels take part in inshore fishing. For political reasons, and because of attempts to conserve diminishing fish stocks, this pattern is in the process of change and many trawlers are laid up.

Stern Trawler

Great improvements were made in working conditions with the introduction of the stern trawler on which the net, with full codend, is hauled inboard through the stern slipway. When the codline is released the catch falls through a hatch to the lower deck where the crew are able to sort, gut and box the fish under cover. This type of trawler is easily distinguished from the conventional side trawler by the stern opening with gantry above and bipod or twin masts from which the derricks and net-handling gear are operated. Furthermore, the stern trawler usually has twin funnels either on the superstructure or separate from it, amidships.

Fig. 94

Stern Trawler built in 1971 with a length of 44·28 m

Freezer trawler and factory ship

On the normal trawler the crew wash and gut the fish, and then pack it on ice in boxes, where it will remain fresh for about fourteen days; the time which a vessel can remain at sea is therefore restricted by this limitation. The freezer trawler can remain at sea for many weeks longer than this as the catch is sorted, washed, gutted and then frozen into about 40-kg blocks and retained at a temperature of about $-28°$ C, until port is reached. The fish is then thawed out and either sold as fresh fish or kept in storage. The fish factory trawler carries the work a stage further

Fig. 95
Freezer factory
stern trawler

twin funnels

gantry

stern ramp

while still at sea. The catch is not only cleaned and gutted, but also filleted, skinned and processed ready for the market. This type of vessel must, therefore, be larger to accommodate the extra machinery refrigerating plant and processing machinery. The greater part of the catch is treated in this way while some is converted into liver oil; offal and small fish are turned into fish meal. **Fig. 95** shows a French vessel with a large refrigerated hold, fish meal and fish oil tanks, a full equipment of headers, filleters and skinners, fully automatic freezing plant, a closed-circuit television to monitor both the fishing operations on deck and the processing below decks.

Fig. 96 Russian
stern-operating fish
factory, 3,050
gross tons

84

Scottish seiner
Fig. 97

2-tonne codend derrick

mizzen sail

A-frames p & s

power block

seine-trawl winch coiler

whaleback   x = fishing lights   10-man liferafts   portable gallows: p & s

Seiner

Seine net fishing was first developed in Scandinavia before the last war. Used by Scottish fishermen during that period, its use has now become widespread. The seine net is shot, and hauled in, over the stern and it is necessary to have a clear space between the wheelhouse and the stern; this is, therefore, a characteristic feature of the seiner. As the warps are being hauled in they are passed forward to a machine, close to the foremast, which coils them neatly on each side of the deck. **Fig. 97** shows the main characteristics of the Scottish seiner and, as this particular vessel is dual purpose, it has the addition of portable steel gallows on the port and starboard quarters for stern trawling. The hydraulic power block, a recent innovation, is now a common feature on even comparatively small fishing boats as it greatly facilitates the handling of the nets. The seiner/trawler shown in the drawing has a length of 22·86 m and a crew of eight. The steel hull has a cruiser stern, a soft-nosed stem and a prominent whaleback, which gives considerable shelter to the men operating the winch and the coiler. Instead of the traditional lifeboat, the vessel carries two of the new type of tenmen liferafts.

85

Fig. 98 Some British motor fishing vessels

a Stern factory trawler, 1,435 g.r.t. with diesel-electric propulsion. **b Distant-water conventional side trawler**, 839 g.r.t. with diesel-electric propulsion and speed of 15 knots, crew of 42, 67 m o.a. **c Small line and lobster boat**, 10 m o.a. **d Distant-water stern trawler***, fish-room capacity of 356 m³, crew of 16, 45 m o.a. **e Inshore stern trawler** with Kort nozzle rudder, 15·24 m o.a. **f Middle-water side trawler**, 280 g.r.t., 40 m o.a. **g Near-water 'pocket' side trawler**, 26·20 m o.a. **h Multi-purpose inshore boat** for pair trawling, side trawling and seining, 24·38 m o.a. **i Drifter** with wooden hull, mizzen sail and cage of floats, or pallets, and rollers along the bulwarks. **j Purse seiner** with power block, also equipped for stern and pair trawling, 26·51 m o.a. **k Near-water stern trawler** with variable pitch propeller, 25 m o.a. **l Brixham trawler** with Rolls-Royce engine, 14 m o.a. **m Inshore multi-purpose fishing vessel** built in 1972 in Orkney and owned in Yorkshire. Glass fibre hull, 16·45 m o.a.

* d Five similar trawlers were converted to minesweepers for the Falklands Task Force.

Fig. 99 Scottish inshore stern trawler operating from the Fife coast

Fig. 100 Some European fishing vessels

a Polish stern freezer trawler, crew of 93 and speed of 12·5 knots. 85 m o.a. **b French deep-sea salt cod trawler** employed on three voyages a year to Newfoundland Banks. Diesel-electric propulsion. 68 m o.a. **c Polish stern trawler** built in 1963. 48 m o.a. **d Spanish pareja** with comparatively high freeboard and clear net platform aft, employed in pair fishing on Newfoundland Banks. 35 m o.a. **e Faroese long liner**, crew of 24 on voyages of 10/12 days' duration laying baited line up to 50 km in length. 36 m o.a. **f Norwegian purse seiner** with characteristic high poop and power block. Frequently seen off Orkney and Shetland. 46 m o.a. **g Portuguese sardine seiner** fishes in coastal waters on two-day trips. 18 m o.a. **h Danish fishing cutter**, crew of six or seven. A sturdy type of vessel capable of fishing in Barents Sea and off Greenland. 30 m o.a. **i Dutch motor-fishing cutter** sometimes fitted with Kort nozzle. 24 m o.a. **j Dutch nearwater fishing cutter** built in 1972. 32 m o.a. **k Spanish tuna purse seiner**, 1972 with facilities for freezing catch. 45 m o.a. **l Norwegian fisheries research trawler** with larger superstructure, and more accommodation, than commercial fishing trawler. 60 m o.a. **m** Forepart of **Norwegian shark-fishing vessel** with harpoon gun on the stem and rope-ladder to crow's nest.

Fig. 101 **a** Norwegian purse seiner   **b** Polish fisheries research vessel

Fig. 102 Some non-European fishing vessels

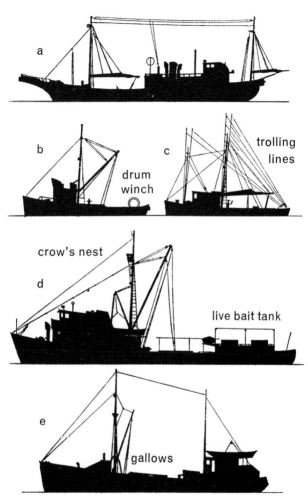

a

b

c

trolling
lines

drum
winch

crow's nest

d

live bait tank

e

gallows

The unusual looking vessel **a** is a modern Japanese mackerel pole and line fisherman. A continuous platform projects from the two sides of the ship right up to the overhanging clipper stem. Live bait is used and during the night fishing sessions powerful lights are hung over the side to attract the fish.

The smaller British Columbian fishing vessel **b** employs two methods of fishing: trolling from poles and lines attached to the foot of the mast and netting by means of a seine net handled over the stern by a powerful drum winch.

The **Pacific troller c** employs the trolling method with two or four rods and steel lines when fishing for salmon off the Pacific coast of North America. A similar method is used by the French tunnymen in the Bay of Biscay. Their rods, or tangons, are about 15 m in length and each one trails six to eight lines.

The **Tuna clipper d** is a 40-m flush-decked launch with a low freeboard used for tuna fishing off the west coast of Mexico, central America and south California. Individual fishermen, each with his own rod, hook and line, fish from a platform which projects all round the hull. Live bait is carried in tanks on the decks close to the stern.

The **New England trawler e** has a length of 23 m and a speed of 9 knots. Working off the eastern seaboard of North America, she makes about twenty trips each year fishing mainly for redfish.

All over the world there are numerous fishing fleets of varying types, but they tend to conform to the main categories already described. The method of fishing employed—whether trawling, drifting, ring netting, seining, long-lining, trolling or rod fishing—will determine their size and characteristics.

The whale factory ship

For many years one of the largest, and most distinctive, merchant ships has been the whale oil factory ship. With high freeboard, twin funnels aft and navigation bridge placed well forward and large stern slipway, she could not be mistaken for any other type. The latest 35,000 gt Russian vessels were capable of dealing with 4,000 whales each trip, but these, and their Japanese counterparts, have become redundant owing to the moratorium of the International Whaling Commission of 1987 ending all large scale commercial whaling. Norway and Iceland will continue to catch a limited number of fin and sei whales for scientific purposes with only local consumption of the whalemeat. Some factory ships have been converted to floating fish factories, and some whalecatchers, or corvettes, are used for other types of fishing. The last British whale factory ship was disposed of in 1963, and a few years later the Norwegians, who had pioneered many of the modern methods of whaling and had dominated the industry for so long, also withdrew their ships.

Fig. 103
The last Dutch whale factory ship, showing the typical stern slipway

Fig. 104 Whale catcher with crow's nest and catwalk, or gunner's bridge

SELECTION OF BRITISH AND IRISH PORT DISTINGUISHING LETTERS

A Aberdeen; AB Aberystwyth; AD Ardrossan;
AH Arbroath; BCK Buckie; BF Banff;
BM Brixham; C Cork; CF Cardiff; CK Colchester;
CS Cowes; CT Castletown; CY Castlebay;
D Dublin; DE Dundee; DH Dartmouth;
DK Dundalk; DO Douglas; FD Fleetwood;
FE Folkestone; FH Falmouth; FR Fraserburgh;
FY Fowey; G Galway; GE Goole; GN Granton;
GU Guernsey; GY Grimsby; H Hull;
HH Harwich; HL Hartlepool; IE Irvine;
INS Inverness; J Jersey; K Kirkwall;
KY Kirkcaldy; LH Leith; LK Lerwick;
LN King's Lynn; LT Lowestoft; LY Londonderry;
M Milford Haven; NN Newhaven; OB Oban;
PD Peterhead; PE Poole; PW Padstow;
PGW Port Glasgow; PZ Penzance; R Ramsgate;
RO Rothesay; S Skibbereen; SA Swansea;
SC Scilly Isles; SE Salcombe; SH Scarborough;
SN Shields, North; SR Stranraer; SS St Ives;
SSS Shields, South; SY Stornoway; T Tralee;
TH Teignmouth; TN Troon; UL Ullapool;
W Waterford; WA Whitehaven; WD Wexford;
WH Weymouth; WK Wick; WN Wigtown;
WY Whitby; Y Yougal; YH Yarmouth

Fig. 105 Research and Diving Support Ship converted from a stern trawler factory ship

Research ship

Two new types of vessel have developed from the stern trawler (**Fig. 94**)—itself a post-war innovation—with the characteristic prominent gantry above a stern slipway. During the extensive development of maritime oil production small submersible craft have been built to undertake sea-bed exploration and to inspect, and repair, the underwater sections of oil rig platforms. These craft need to be attended by Diving Support mother ships and the gantry is therefore necessary to lift the submersible to and from the ship's hold.

The other type resembling the stern trawler is the fisheries or oceanographical research ship. The former is well represented by the *Profesor Siedlecki* (**Fig. 101b**) belonging to the Polish Fisheries Institute and employed on research all over the world. Many governments have a number of fisheries research ships for study over a wide range of ocean and inshore waters. The Royal Research Ship *Challenger* (**Fig. 106**) is one of twenty or so vessels belonging to the National Environment Council for hydrographic, geological, magnetic or biological research. Each vessel has accommodation for a group of

Fig. 106
RRS
Challenger
Br/1972/
1440 disp/
54·86 m/10·5 k

scientists and laboratories, workshops and special deck machinery according to the work in hand.

4 FLAGS

International Code (Fig. 107)

The present version of the International Code of Signals came into being in 1934 and was revised in April 1969. The Royal Navy has its own code, although many of the same flags are used.

Signal letters

In addition to the letter values shown in **Plate 1**, each flag has a signal value. For example, the letter **D** also means 'Keep clear of me—I am manoeuvring with difficulty.' Every ship, and even many small yachts, has a four-letter identification signal. British ships have either **G** or **M** as the first letter. The letter **F** represents France, **PA** or **PI** Holland, and **K**, **N** or **W** the United States of America.

Every phrase likely to be used at sea is represented by a group of code letters. Each ship carries the official International Code books which contain all these recognized signals. If it is necessary to send an unusual signal, perhaps containing someone's name, the words may be spelt out letter by letter. To economize in flags, substitute flags are used; for instance, in the signal indicating the port of Plymouth, **AMPM**, the last letter would be indicated by a second substitute flag instead of another **M**.

Signals flags should always be flown from a point where they can be read without obstruction from masts or stays. If more than one point is used the signal reads from forward aft.

On festive occasions in port, ships of all types may 'dress ship', that is, fly all the code flags on a taut line hoisted from the stem or bowsprit over the trucks of the masts down to the stern.

Signal Flags: Selection of Signals

A I have a diver down; keep well clear at slow speeds.
B I am taking in, or discharging, or carrying explosives. **C** Yes (*Affirmative*). **D** Keep clear of me—I am manoeuvring with difficulty. **E** I am altering my course to starboard. **F** I am disabled. **G** I require a pilot (for *Fishing Vessels*—I am hauling nets). **H** I have a pilot on board. **I** I am altering my course to port. **J** I am on fire and have dangerous cargo on board—keep well clear of me. **K** I wish to communicate with you. **L** You should stop your vessel instantly. **M** My vessel is stopped and making no way through the water. **N** No (*Negative*). **O** Man overboard. **P** (*Blue Peter*) *In harbour:* All persons are to repair on board as the vessel is about to proceed to sea (*flown at the foremast*). *At sea it may be used by fishing boats to mean:* My nets have come fast upon an obstruction. **Q** My vessel is healthy. I request a free pratique. (*A vessel arriving in British waters from abroad must declare whether she is 'Healthy' or 'Suspect'. Pratique is permission to hold intercourse with the port. If there is a case of infectious disease on board, the signal* **QQ** *is hoisted signifying* My ship is suspect.)* **S** My engines are going astern. **T** Keep clear of me: I am engaged in pair trawling. **U** You are running into danger. **V** I require assistance. **W** I require medical assistance. **X** Stop carrying out your intentions and watch for my signals. **Y** I am dragging my anchor. **Z** I require a tug. *When made by fishing vessels operating in close proximity on the fishing-grounds* I am shooting nets. **Selection of two-letter signals: AM** Have you a doctor? **NC** I am in distress and require immediate assistance.

---

* No signal allocated to letter R.

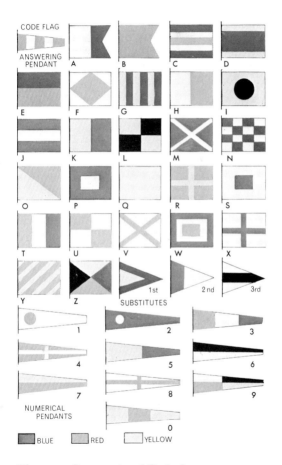

Fig. 107 International Code flags

1 U.K. RED ENSIGN 2 FRANCE 3 NETHERLANDS

4 U.K. BLUE ENSIGN 5 BELGIUM 6 ITALY

7 CANADA 8 SPAIN 9 FINLAND

10 U.S.A. 11 PORTUGAL 12 SWEDEN

13 LIBERIA 14 WEST GERMANY 15 POLAND

16 EIRE 17 GREECE 18 U.S.S.R.

19 JAPAN 20 DENMARK 21 NORWAY 22 PANAMA

Nos. 9,12 & 17 – Light Blue   Blue   Red   Yellow

Fig. 108 Merchant flags and ensigns (1)

Merchant Flags (Figs. 108 and 110)

Countries and governments are represented by national flags, and in many instances the merchant flag, worn by all types of merchant ship and pleasure craft, is identical. The merchant flag is worn at a vessel's stern on the ensign staff and is frequently referred to as an ensign. In port, merchant flags are hoisted at 8 a.m. between March and September, and at 9 a.m. between September and March; they are hauled down at sunset. They must be worn when a ship is entering or leaving port at any time of the day or night. British ships of over fifty tons are compelled by law to carry or wear their national merchant flags. **Fig. 109** shows the position at which various flags are worn.

British Ensigns

The RED ENSIGN (**Fig. 108** No. 1) is the flag of the Merchant Navy worn by all British-owned mer-

Fig. 109 Positions of flags worn by merchant ships and warships

Fig. 110 Merchant flags and ensigns

1 R.N. White Ensign
2 Royal Fleet Aux. Serv.
3 Trinity House
4 Royal Air Force
5 Lifeboat Serv.
6 Northern Lights
7 G.B. Union Flag
Colour Key
RED
BLUE
GREEN
ORANGE
YELLOW
8 Irish Lights
9 NEW ZEALAND
10 R.N. Vice-Admiral
11 AUSTRALIA
12 EGYPT (U.A.R)
13 ISRAEL
14 SOUTH AFRICA
15 Chinese Republic
16 INDIA
17 PAKISTAN
18 ARGENTINA
19 BRAZIL
20 CHILE

chant, pleasure or private craft. The BLUE ENSIGN
(**Fig. 108** No. 4) is worn as the merchant flag by
British ships having among their crew a certain
number of officers and men belonging to the Royal
Naval Reserve. Many yacht clubs use it defaced by
their club emblems. Lloyd's, Customs, and some
other institutions also wear this flag with their badges
in the fly, and the Royal Army Service Corps vessels
wear a blue ensign with crossed swords. The WHITE
ENSIGN (**Fig. 110** No. 1) is the ensign of the Royal
Navy and is worn by all HM ships, shore establish-
ments and boats of the Royal Yacht Squadron. Ships
of the ROYAL FLEET AUXILIARY SERVICE wear a blue
ensign defaced by a gold anchor (**Fig. 110** No. 2).
ROYAL AIR FORCE stations, air sea rescue launches
and other vessels use a pale blue ensign with the well-
known roundel (**Fig. 110** No. 4). Lifeboat stations fly
the flag of the ROYAL NATIONAL LIFEBOAT INSTITU-
TION (**Fig. 110** No. 5) and the lifeboats wear a red
ensign with a small version of the flag on the fly.
Lighthouse tenders in Scotland and the Isle of Man
belonging to the COMMISSIONERS OF NORTHERN
LIGHTS wear a blue ensign, but when the commissioners are on board a tender a white ensign (**Fig.
110** No. 6) is worn. UNION FLAG (**Fig. 110** No. 7) is
worn at the jackstaff of British warships at anchor or
alongside a quay. The pilot flag is a Union flag with
a white border, known as the Union Jack, and worn
at the jackstaff by merchant ships, or at the foremast
when a pilot is required. The Union flag is quite
commonly, but incorrectly, referred to as the *Union
Jack*. **Fig. 110** No. 10 shows the Royal Navy
COMMAND flag flown by a Vice-Admiral.

The merchant flags of India and Pakistan are red
with the national flags (Nos. 16 & 17) in the canton,
i.e. the upper quarter next to the staff.

Flags of convenience

Since the 1940s an increasing number of European and American shipowners have registered some of their merchant ships in small countries which do not themselves have significant merchant fleets. At present about one third of the world's merchant fleets are registered in countries under 'flags of convenience' or, to use the American term, 'flags of necessity'.

The main reason for this practice is that the shipowners pay little or no tax on profits from ships thus registered. Furthermore the 'convenience' countries have more relaxed regulations with regard to safety, and inspection, and the qualifications, experience and wages of the officers and men may be of a lower standard. In some vessels the standards of efficiency are equal to those of the parent countries but there are many cases to the contrary.

The largest number of vessels are registered in Panama (**Fig. 108** No. 22) and Liberia (No. 13) and those of the latter have the name Monrovia painted on the stern as home port. Other countries concerned, to a much lesser degree, are Costa Rica, Honduras, Taiwan, the Philippine Republic, and an increasing number, Singapore. Some British ships are registered in the Bahamas or Bermuda and an example of the latter is the Cunard cruise liner *Cunard Princess*.

Recently Gibraltar and the Isle of Man have been included in the ever increasing flags of convenience. By the end of 1986 only half the number of British owned merchant ships were registered on the UK mainland and consequently still wear the once ubiquitous 'red duster' (**Fig. 108** No. 1).

By courtesy of P & O

Fig. 111

Cruise Liner *Royal Princess* built in Finland in 1984 for world-wide cruising based on Los Angeles. All 1,200 passengers are accommodated in outside cabins with picture windows. Propulsion is by diesel engines driving twin controllable-pitch propellers giving a maximum speed of 22 knots. The ship has an overall length of 232 metres and measures 44,348 gross tonnage.

By courtesy of Jim Prentice

Fig. 112
Semi-submersible heavy lift cargo vessel *Mighty Servant 1*. Built in 1983, this unusual looking vessel belongs to the famous Dutch towage and salvage company of Wijsmuller. Nearly 20,000 tonnes gross, she has an overall length of 160 metres and is propelled by diesel-electric machinery. In April 1986 Captain Scott's research vessel *Discovery* was carried from London to Dundee on board a semi-submersible similar to that in Fig. 19.

FotoFlite, Ashford

Fig. 113
British Container Ship *Andes* of 32,150 gt built in 1984 for Furness Withy. The travelling gantry, running the full length of the weather deck, is fitted with a swivelling extension in order to lift the boxes outboard. With an overall length of 202 metres, she has a capacity for 2145 TEU (TEU = twenty-foot equivalent units) containers (page 34).

FotoFlite, Ashford

Fig. 114

Bulk Carrier *British Steel*. Built by Harland & Wolff in Belfast in 1984 this 173,000 dwt ship is the largest bulk carrier to be built in Europe. With an overall length of 287 metres, her diesel engines give her a maximum speed of 13·6 knots (page 48).

By courtesy of Sealink British Ferries

Fig. 115
Passenger and Car Ferry *St Christopher*. Two French and two British passenger-car ferries run on the 90-minute crossing between Dover and Calais. One of the British ships, *St Christopher*, was built in 1981 with accommodation for 1,400 passengers and 310 cars, and has a maximum speed of 19·5 knots (page 59).

FotoFlite, Ashford

Fig. 116
Vehicle Carrier *Höegh Trader*. Built in 1982 in Gdynia, this PCTC is owned by the Norwegian company of Leif Höegh which possesses a large fleet of bulk carriers and container ships as well as vehicle carriers. The stern ramps leading to the car deck are raised and her single square funnel is right aft on the starboard side (page 51).

By courtesy of Silja Line

Fig. 117

For a time *Finlandia* and her sistership *Silvia Regina* were the world's largest passenger/car ferries but they have now been outclassed by several others such as the huge vessels on the UK-Netherlands route (page 57). Built in 1981, *Finlandia* has a length of 166 metres to accommodate 2,000 passengers, at a maximum speed of 20 knots on the 27-hour run between Helsinki and Stockholm.

FotoFlite, Ashford

Fig. 118

Barge carrier *Baco-Liner 3*. This new type of barge carrier has loading doors at the bows for float-in facilities and a gantry crane running the full length of the weather deck. Cargo capacity is for 501 TEU containers (TEU = twenty-foot equivalent units) and 12 lighters. This German vessel has two sister ships and, completed in 1984, she well represents this new type of ocean-going vessel, which has developed in only 16 years (page 52). The Soviet Union is now building a fleet of nuclear-powered vessels of this type carrying seventy-four 450-tonne barges.

By courtesy of G. Heath, Trinity House

Fig. 119
The Trinity House Vessel *Patricia*, based on Harwich, is the largest of the service's fleet of district tenders. Of 2,540 gt and a length of 86·5 metres, her diesel-electric propulsion gives her a speed of 14 knots (page 72). THV *Mermaid* was commissioned in 1987.

Fig. 120
RASing—Refuelling warships at sea. A 36,000 gt Royal Fleet Auxiliary of the *Ol* class fuelling two warships underway (see page 157). On the replenishment ship's port beam is one of the *Invincible* class aircraft carriers with a number of VTOL Sea Harriers and Sea King helicopters on the flight deck. On her starboard beam is the amphibious assault ship HMS *Fearless* whose unusually placed funnels can be seen as well as her spacious flight deck for helicopters for the Royal Marine Commando units.

6 WARSHIPS

General Characteristics

Colour In all countries naval vessels are painted grey. Ships of the Royal Navy are painted light grey, with white topmasts if they are in commission; in reserve, the topmasts are painted grey. On service in certain eastern waters the ships are painted white. All British submarines are painted black. **General appearance** The warship's long, low outline is broken by gun houses and controls, with the main superstructure building up near or around the foremast. This mast, and the mainmast or tower, has a large number of radar antennae and aerials, and unlike the cargo ship the warship never has a raised poop. She is generally flush decked and may have a long forecastle deck which extends well aft. Some frigates have a raised forecastle, but this is quite distinct from that of a cargo liner. **Propulsion** Most

---

Fig. 121 Parts of a Warship. Ex-British 'County' class guided missile destroyer. **a** and **b** 115-mm-radar-controlled fully automatic dual-purpose quick-firing guns in twin turrets. **f** forecastle. **js** jackstaff. **n** navigating bridge. **gr** gun control radar. **sr** search radar. **sh** signal halyards. **t** topmast. **awr** air warning search radar. **l** launches and inflatable rafts. **sc** close-range anti-aircraft missile launcher. **mr** missile guidance radar. **h** helicopter landing deck. **ss** medium-range guided missile launcher. **q** quarter deck. **es** ensign staff. (Note: these ships have been sold to other navies.)

fighting ships are propelled by high pressure steam turbines and oil-fired water-tube boilers. Although now common for merchant ships, diesel engines are much less used for warships. Some frigates, most minesweepers and patrol vessels do have motor engines, and the latter can be combined with gas turbines—CODOG propulsion. Gas turbines have been introduced in several classes of vessel in various combinations. COGOG indicates that a ship has two sets of gas turbines—one for full power and the other for cruising. COSAG combines geared steam turbines and gas turbines. Nuclear-powered steam turbine vessels have been in operation for some years. In the Royal Navy this method is confined to ballistic missile and fleet submarines, but in the United States Navy some aircraft carriers, missile cruisers and missile frigates are propelled in this way, as well as ballistic missile and attack submarines. **Protection** The battleship was protected amidships by armour plating up to 400 mm in thickness, but the average armour used on present-day ships is very much thinner. Cruisers were built with some protection at water-line and round certain vital parts of the ship, but destroyers, frigates and other warships have no additional protection at all. **Subdivision of the hull** Another difference between the structure of a cargo vessel and that of a fighting ship is that the former hull is divided into six or eight large compartments by watertight transverse bulkheads. On the other hand the warship, with no large cargo holds, is divided by many transverse and longitudinal watertight bulkheads into a great number of small compartments; these can be sealed off by watertight doors if there has been flooding by accident or naval action. **Tonnage** refers to Full Load Displacement; standard tonnage is approximately one fifth less.

Calibre or length	Mountings or other characteristics	Type of warship
Guns 4·5 in. (115 mm)	Single or twin mounting in armoured turrets; fully automatic radar controlled. Dual purpose AA	Destroyers; Types 22 and 23 and *Leander* class frigates
40 mm	Bofors guns. Mounting of 1, 2 or 6 barrels. Open or light shields. High speed close-range AA guns. May be fully automatic and radar controlled	Standard for all fighting ships and auxiliaries
20 mm	Oerlikon—single mounting heavy machine guns	Light AA guns for most vessels
Guided Missiles *Polaris* 9·45 m	Thermo-nuclear inter-continental ballistic missile; range up to 2,500 miles. By the 1990s a new generation of submarines will be equipped with US *Trident II* multihead missiles with almost twice the range of *Polaris*	*Resolution* class submarines
Exocet 5·21 m	All weather surface-to-surface missile (French SMM missile)	Types 21 and 22 frigates
Sea Dart 4·36 m	Medium range surface-to-air missile. Twin launchers	Destroyers and aircraft carriers; Types 22 and 23 frigate
Seawolf 2 m	Close-in air defence missiles	*Broadsword* Fs
Seacat 1·48 m	Short-range anti-aircraft missiles. To be replaced by Sea Wolf	Assault ships, *Amazon*, *Leander*
Torpedoes *Harpoon* 4·58 m	Long-range anti-ship torpedo	Types 22 and 23 frigates; *Swiftsure* class submarines
Tigerfish 6·4 m	Heavyweight anti-submarine torpedoes	Nuclear powered submarines
21 in (diam)	Lightweight anti-submarine torpedoes. Triple mounts. Stingray—new development	Type 42 destroyers, *Broadsword*, *Amazon* & some *Leander* Fs
Depth Charges or Mortors	Long barrelled triple launchers. Automatic depth charge setting	Some frigates

The armament of all warships is under constant review as new weapons systems and other technical developments are introduced.

Comparative profiles of ships of the Royal Navy

Fig. 122

scale

10 0 10 20 30 40 50 60 70 80

metres

Notes: figures in brackets give total numbers of ships in the class, including: operational, reserve, training and refitting. April 1989.

Aircraft Carriers page 123

    a HMS *Hermes*. Sold to India 1986

    b *Invincible* class (3) Multi-purpose role

Guided Missile Destroyers page 139

    c County class. Sold to other navies

    d HMS *Bristol* (1) General purpose ship

    e *Sheffield* class, Type 42 (13) Area air defence; name *Sheffield* now transferred to a Type 22 Frigate

Frigates page 143

    f *Broadsword* class. Type 22 (14) Anti-submarine

    g *Amazon* class. Type 21 (6) General purpose

    h *Leander* class (15) Anti-submarine role. Includes Exocet and broadbeamed groups

Submarines page 147

    i *Resolution* class (4) Nuclear powered; Strategic power projection; Polaris missiles

    j *Valiant* class (5) Nuclear power; hunter-killer

    k *Swiftsure* class (6) and *Trafalgar* (6) class Nuclear power; hunter-killer

    l *Oberon* (11) and *Upholder* class (1) Patrol

Mine Counter Measure Ships page 149

    m HMS *Abdiel* Paid off during 1988

    n 'Ton' class minesweepers/hunters (15)

    o 'Hunt' class mine disposal ships (13) (12 River class)

Non-Combatant Ships

    p HMS *Britannia* (1) Royal Yacht/hospital ship

    q HMS *Endurance* (1) Ice patrol ship, hydro- and oceanographic survey in South Atlantic

    r *Bulldog* class survey vessel (3) page 155

    s *Hecla* class survey vessel (3)

Patrol Craft page 154

    t Island class patrol craft (7) Offshore patrol and fishery protection

Assault Ships page 135

    u HMS *Fearless* and HMS *Intrepid* (2) Amphibious warfare and support ships

Fig. 123 HMS *Swiftsure* is a development of the nuclear powered *Valiant* class of hunter-killer submarine. The boats in this class have a length of 83 metres and an underwater displacement of 4,500 tonnes and a maximum speed of 30 knots submerged. The armament consists of 5 heavy weight torpedo tubes or Harpoon long range anti ship missiles torpedo tubes and the latest air conditioning and purification plants enable the submarine to undertake patrols of long endurance at high speeds without the need to surface for fresh air.

Fig. 124 HMS *Boxer* is one of the Batch 2 'stretched' Type 22 frigates with a displacement of 4,400 tonnes and a length of 146 metres. Not only are these ships larger than the earlier all metric *Broadsword* class but they are equipped with a much more advanced all-missile weapons system. They are powered by gas turbines and have controllable pitch propellers and stabiliser fins. The photograph shows the hangars for the two anti-submarine Lynx helicopters which can be armed with homing torpedoes or depth charges.

P. A. Vicary

Fig. 125   Guided Missile Destroyer HMS *Bristol*

Pennant Letters of British Warships

R Aircraft carriers or commando carriers. **S** Submarines. **L** Assault ships, logistic landing ships and landing craft. **C** Cruisers. **D** Destroyers. **F** Frigates. **N** Minelayers. **K** Helicopter support ships. **M** Minesweepers—coastal and inshore. **P** Seaward defence boats, boom defence vessels, coastal patrol and fast patrol vessels. **A** Support ships and auxiliaries.

Fig. 126   Aircraft carrier HMS *Invincible*—designed as a command centre for maritime forces and for the operation of helicopters and VTOL/STOL

aircraft. The 'ski-jump' and Sea Dart missile launchers are seen at the forward end of the flight deck.

Fig. 127   Flight deck of a fixed wing aircraft carrier

Aircraft Carrier

The aircraft carrier is easily recognized by her size and the immense, clear deck with neither camber nor sheer, which stretches the full length and width of the ship. The funnel, control tower and navigating bridge form a narrow island superstructure on the starboard side. The search and aircraft direction radars, and other aerials on either lattice masts or towers are also situated on the superstructure. The carrier has no offensive weapons but is equipped with a few 115-mm and/or quadruple surface-to-air missile launchers. The service speed of the bigger carriers is between 30 and 35 knots; in all cases the ships are propelled by geared turbines. The flight deck, hangars and machinery spaces are protected by armour plating up to 100 mm in thickness, and round the hull, at the water-line, is a belt of armour slightly more than that in thickness. The flight deck of a fixed wing aircraft carrier is now always set at an angle of about 8° from the centre line. This British invention increases the efficiency of the aircraft on landing, and gives parking space forward of the superstructure. Aircraft are assisted in take-off by steam catapults—another British invention. Aircraft are normally stowed in hangars below the flight deck with access by either centre-line or side lifts.

a

b

c

d

e

Fig. 128 Aircraft carriers

Aircraft Carriers

a *Kiev* class carriers—three ships and one building. 37,000 tonnes, 274 m, 32 knots. Armed with a variety of missile systems and ten torpedo tubes. Operate about 40 VTOL and helicopters. **b** French *Clemenceau* (and *Foch*) 1961/32,780 tonnes/265 m/Steam turbines and twin screws/24 knots service speed. With a capacity for 40 aircraft, this vessel has a defensive armament of eight 100-mm automatic guns in single turrets. **c** Italian light carrier *Guiseppe Garibaldi* 1985/13,320 t full load/180 m/CGOG/30 k. VTOL aircraft, helicopters, mixed missile launchers, torpedo tubes. **d** French PA75 (building), nuclear-powered carrier, laid down in 1981, 18,000 t full load/ 202 m/28 k. Unique design with accommodation for 1,000/1,500 passengers and three hospital wards equipped to deal with natural and other disasters during peace-time. **e** British *Invincible* class carrier 19,500 t full load/206 m/COGAG/28 k VTOL aircraft, helicopters. Variously classified as 'through deck cruiser', 'mini-aircraft carrier' and latterly 'aircraft carrier'. Designed for multi-purpose role including fleet defence and anti-submarine work. By the 1990s the US Navy will have fifteen aircraft carriers in commission and seven of these will be nuclear powered. The USSR 64,000 tonne *Tbilisi* will soon be in service with a sister ship now building. During the last war the RN possessed a number of light carriers of the *Colossus* and similar classes and a number of these were purchased later by other navies. Two of these only are still operational: *Minas Gerais* of Brazil, and *25 de Mayo* of Argentina—both considerably modernised in recent years.

Fig. 129 Nuclear-powered attack carrier USS *Enterprise* 1961/89,600 tonnes/341·3 m/35 k. The first nuclear-powered warship and the largest warship ever built, about equalled by the more recent *Nimitz* class carriers. She carries about 100 fixed wing aircraft and has four steam catapults and four lifts giving access to the hangars. The nuclear reactor unit for providing steam to the turbines requires no funnel uptakes, therefore the superstructure is small and less vulnerable to air attack. For defence she is equipped with short-range supersonic anti-aircraft missiles.

Fig. 130 The 20-metre overhang of the flight deck and side lift of USS *Forrestal* 1955/78,000 tonnes/80 aircraft

Cruiser

Until the period shortly after the Second World War, the term *cruiser* was used to define a clearly understood type of fighting ship divided into two categories: *heavy* cruisers with a main armament of eight-inch (203-mm) guns and *light* cruisers equipped with six-inch (152-mm) guns. Although it was gun power rather than size which determined the category, the heavy cruiser was usually in the 10/14,000 tonnes range, while the light cruiser was often as small as 4,500 tonnes displacement.

The duties of the cruiser were many: she had to protect seaborne trade routes by escorting convoys, search for and attack commerce raiders, give protection from aircraft and submarines, and form part of a defensive screen for larger warships such as aircraft carriers and battleships. For these duties she had to be equipped with a diversity of weapons; she had to be fast, and she had to be designed for spending long periods at sea without refuelling. Some of the wartime United States heavy cruisers remain converted to missile cruisers, and a small number retain their original gun armament as potential Fire Support Ships in reserve. Many light cruisers have similarly been converted, partially or wholly, for the use of guided missiles: surface-to-air guided missiles and new anti-submarine weapons that replace the traditional guns. The USSR is believed to be building two nuclear-powered battle-cruisers and a number of gun/missile cruisers to add to their fleet of 6-in cruisers.

Guided Missile Cruiser

The guided missile cruiser may be either a converted gun cruiser or a purpose-built vessel. Some cruisers retain a small number of conventional guns, but the main armament consists of surface-to-air and AS missile launchers. The largest ship in this category is the USS *Long Beach* (**Fig. 134**), a nuclear-powered ship of 14,200 tonnes standard displacement, built in 1961. Her armament consists of three twin surface-to-air launchers, an eight tube AS launcher, two triple tube torpedo units and two single 127-mm dual-purpose AA guns. **a** United States *Albany* class 1940s¹ 13,700 tonnes/205·3 m/ST/33 k converted in the 1960s from orthodox heavy cruisers armed with 203-mm (8-in) guns. The very tall funnels and high control tower are quite distinctive. Armament consists of four surface-to-air launchers, two triple torpedo tubes and two 127-mm guns. **b** United States *California* class 1973/10,000 tonnes/181·7 m/Nuclear power ST/30 knots. Officially referred to as a frigate in USA nomenclature, it is in all respects, i.e. armament, speed and size, similar to the guided missile cruiser of other nations. **c** Russian *Kresta II* class 1970/7,600 tonnes/158 m/ST/33 k. Armament consists of surface-to-surface and surface-to-air launchers, AS weapons and ten torpedo tubes. The superstructure amidships is even more festooned with radar scanners and aerials than the normal up-to-date warship. Aft of the after missile launcher is a helideck and hangar for a single helicopter. **d** Peruvian *Aguirre* (ex-Netherlands navy). 1953/12,165 tonnes/188·7 m/ST/32 k. Built as an all-gun cruiser she has been converted to a guided missile cruiser with a mixed armament and a strong bias towards conventional gunnery. She has a twin missile launcher aft, but four twin turret 152-mm guns and a large number of 57-mm and 40-mm AA guns.

Fig. 131   Guided missile cruisers

Fig. 132 French cruiser *Colbert* with conventional guns forward and guided missile launchers aft

Fig. 133 Nuclear-powered guided missile cruiser USS *Mississippi*

Fig. 134 Nuclear-powered cruiser USS *Long Beach*

Fig. 135 HMS *Southampton*, commissioned in 1981, is one of the standard *Sheffield* class destroyers with a displacement tonnage of 4,100 full load and a length of 125 metres. She is armed with one 115 mm (4·5 in) dual purpose gun forward, Sea Dart surface-to-air missiles, Oerlikon AA guns, and six anti-submarine torpedo tubes. Powered by gas turbines, the maximum speed is 29 knots and a range of 4,000 miles at 18 knots. The 1983 onwards ships of the class have a 'stretched' length of 139 metres. One Westland Lynx helicopter is carried, with a hangar aft.

A good example of a British all-gun heavy cruiser has now been preserved as a permanent exhibit. HMS *Belfast* is berthed in the Thames, opposite the Tower of London, and is open to the public. As the largest cruiser of the Second World War, she was completed by Harland and Wolff in 1939 with a full load displacement of 14,930 tonnes. Her armament consists of twelve six-inch (152-mm) guns in triple turrets, and a number of 40-mm AA guns. When she was refitted in 1959 her torpedo tubes were removed and the tripod masts were replaced by lattice structures. The cruiser will be remembered for the important part she played in the Battle of North Cape, in December 1943, when the German battleship *Scharnhorst* was destroyed while attempting to intercept a Russia-bound Allied convoy. In the action with HMS *Belfast* were the battleship HMS *Duke of York*, the heavy cruiser HMS *Norfolk*, two light cruisers, HMS *Sheffield* and *Jamaica*, and eight destroyers.

Fig. 136 HMS *Belfast* at her permanent berth near Tower Bridge

P. A. Vicary

Fig. 137
French
helicopter
cruiser
*Jeanne
d'Arc*

Fig. 138 Italian helicopter
cruiser *Vittorio Veneto*

*By courtesy of
Italian Naval Attaché*

Fig. 139 Helicopter cruisers

Helicopter Cruisers

Although many warships of different types are now equipped with a helicopter-landing platform, the helicopter cruiser is quite distinctive. The high flight deck is an unobstructed area extending to between one-third and one-half of the full length of the vessel.

Fig. 139 a Italian *Vittorio Veneto* 1969/9,500 tonnes/ 179 m/ST/30·5 k. Designed as a multi-purpose ship, she carries a squadron of nine helicopters and is armed with a twin surface-to-air missile launcher forward, eight 76-mm guns and torpedo tubes. **b** Italian *Andrea Doria* class guided missile escort cruiser 1964/5,000 tonnes/149·3 m/30 k is a smaller version of **a** with a similar armament but much smaller flight deck. **c** Russian *Moskva* class helicopter missile cruiser 1967/17,000 tonnes/190·5 m/ST/30 k. Very unconventional in appearance, this vessel can carry up to 30 helicopters and is armed with surface-to-air and anti-submarine missiles. The enormous funnel forms the mainmast and major part of the bridge superstructure. **d** French *Jeanne d'Arc* 1964/ 10,000 tonnes/182 m/ST/26·5 k eight helicopters and armed with four 100-mm guns, two of which are placed at the stern.

helicopter deck

a

funnels

entrance to dock
compartment

bridge on
starboard side

35-tonne
cranes

b

c

34-metre
bow ramp

staggered
uneven funnels

vehicle deck

stern gate

d

Fig. 140   Assault landing ships

Assault Landing Ships

a HMS *Fearless* and *Intrepid* 1965–7/12,120 tonnes/ 158·5 m/ST/21 k. With a full load this type of ship can carry four landing craft on davits, four landing craft (mechanized) in the dock, fifteen tanks and a number of heavy vehicles on the helicopter deck. There is accommodation for 350 troops, as well as a crew of over 500, including military engineers, and communications units. As multi-purpose ships they can serve as naval and brigade headquarters in a seaborne assault operation, carry assault troops and their armour, and offer maintenance facilities for other vessels. **b** French *Orage* 1968/8,500 tonnes/ 149 m/M/17 k. This assault ship and her sister, fulfil the same purpose as **a** and have similar facilities for carrying landing craft, tanks and troops. An unusual feature is the narrow bridge placed on the starboard side as on aircraft carriers. **c** USS *Blue Ridge* 1970/ 19,290 tonnes full load/188·5 m/ST/20 k. This amphibious command ship, with the high freeboard and continuous deck, resembles an aircraft carrier. Her duty is to act as command and control centre in an assault which involves sea, land, air and amphibious forces. Conspicuous are the numerous radar towers and aerials. **d** USS *Newport* 1969/8,342 tonnes full load/159·2 m/M/20 k. One of a large series of tank landing craft with a higher speed than earlier types. Instead of a hinged bow door forward, similar to those used in craft of the last war, a bow ramp is hinged at deck level and operated by derricks which project over the stem. At the stern, a gate allows vehicles to pass from the tank direct to water level. Like **a**, the two funnels are *en echelon*, but in this case they are also different in width.

Fig. 141
French guided
missile destroyer
Duquesne

*By courtesy of
French Naval
Attaché*

Fig. 142 Swedish destroyer *Östergötland* with
mixed armament of conventional guns and guided
missile launchers   *By courtesy of Swedish Naval Attaché*

Fig. 143 Nuclear-powered guided missile frigate
USS *Truxton*   *Official US Navy photograph*

Destroyers

In the 1890s the need arose for a fast, well-armed and seaworthy vessel to counteract the torpedo-boat, and the shipbuilding firm of Yarrow designed such a boat which proved a great success. Known as a *torpedo-boat destroyer* her functions gradually broadened, and eventually the term was simplified to *destroyer*, as she became an important multi-purpose unit in every fleet. Size, speed and armament increased, and during the Second World War many destroyers reached the 2,000-tonne mark with guns of light cruiser calibre.

The term destroyer persists but now it has no particular meaning; it is usually given to a class of fighting ship smaller, but much faster, than a cruiser with a mixed armament of all, or some, of the following weapons: orthodox guns, surface-to-air and surface-to-surface guided missiles, AS homing missiles, conventional torpedoes and depth-charge mortars. As before, the destroyer's duties are many, and she may be employed as an escort giving powerful AA and AS protection, take part in surface action with similar forces, or give support to landing operations. Some of the guided missile armed destroyers are designed so that in the event of contamination by radio-active material they can be completely washed down. Most previously all-gun destroyers are gradually being refitted with at least one guided missile launcher. Some ex-British and ex-United States Navy wartime destroyers still operate in Commonwealth and other navies, and some are in reserve. The RN 'C' class destroyer *Cavalier* (1944) has been preserved as a museum ship.

Fig. 144   Guided missile destroyers

a

115-mm gun
sea dart
helicopter deck

b

115-mm gun
ikara launcher
twin funnels
sea dart
limbo mortar

c

127-mm gun
ikara launcher
127-mm gun
tartar launcher

d

100-mm guns
radar dome
missile launcher

e

127-mm gun
SAM launchers
Y-funnel
hangar for 2 helicopters
torpedo tubes
limbo depth charge mortars

f

missile launchers
a/s launcher
torpedo tubes
gas exhaust casing
76-mm guns

Guided Missile Destroyers

Fig. 144 a HMS *Sheffield** 1972/4,250 tonnes full load/125 m/COGOG/30 k. 'Type 42' class gas turbine ships—one set for full power and one for cruising. Armed with one 115-mm gun, twin 'Sea Dart' surface-to-air missile launcher, two 20-mm AA guns, AS torpedoes launched by helicopter. **b** HMS *Bristol* 1972/6,750 tonnes/154·5 m/COSAG/30 k. 'Type 82' propelled by combined steam and gas turbines. One 115-mm gun, one 'Sea Dart' missile launcher. Unusual with three funnels. **c** Royal Australian Navy *Perth* class 1968/4,500 tonnes/132·2 m/ST/35 k. Armed with 'Tartar' surface-to-air and 'Ikara' anti-submarine missile launchers, two triple torpedo tubes. Built in the USA and similar in design to US destroyers. **d** French guided missile leader *Duquesne* 1969/6,090 tonnes/157·6 m/ST/34 k. Easily distinguished by the radome. Armed with surface-to-air missile launchers and AS homing torpedo launcher and tubes. **e** Canadian 'Tribal' class vessel *Huron* 4,200 tonnes displacement. 129 m. oa. propelled by gas turbines and a speed of 30 knots. Designed for anti-submarine duties with ship-to-air and ship-to-ship missiles. Distinctive simple profile, prominent helicopter hangar and unusual Y funnel (**Fig. 146**). **f** Russian *Krivak* class 1971/4,000 tonnes/123·4 m/GT/38 k. Armed with surface-to-air and AS rocket launchers, eight conventional torpedo tubes and four 76-mm guns. One distinguishing feature is the squat gas exhaust casing which does not resemble any other type of ship's funnel.

* The name ship and HMS *Coventry* were lost in the Falklands.

Frigates

In the early nineteenth century a frigate was described as 'a light nimble ship built for the purpose of sailing swiftly'. The term, however, went out of use until after the last war, when it was found that the corvette was too small and the conventional destroyer had ceased to serve its original purpose. As a result, destroyers became specialist AA or AS ships and smaller, lighter versions with similar functions were developed and known as frigates. Since then the specialist frigates have given way to more general purpose ships. In the Royal Navy, and many other navies, the frigate is primarily intended for fast escort duties and is equipped with AA and AS armament, and long-range detection gear. In the US Navy, however, the term frigate is applied to a ship above 5,000 tonnes with armament more akin to that of the light cruiser. The nuclear-powered guided missile frigates USS *Bainbridge* and *California* class are examples. The French 6,090-tonne ships of the *Suffren* class are known as *frégates lance-engins*, and many of the same country's frigate-type ships are known as escorts.

The modern frigate is then a fast ship with a mixed armament of guns, missiles and torpedoes, designed to outpace nuclear submarines and to do many duties in connection with fleet and convoy escort. In 1968 HMS *Exmouth*, built in 1957 as an anti-submarine frigate, was converted to gas turbine power and became the first warship to be thus propelled. Since then new British destroyers and frigates have been designed with the COGOG system of propulsion, i.e. complete gas turbines as compared with the ships of some foreign navies building CODOG—combined diesel and gas turbine-propulsion.

Fig. 145 British *Leander* class
general purpose frigate

Crown copyright

Fig. 146 HMS *Norfolk*, Duke class frigate
(Type 23)

By courtesy of Jim Prentice

Fig. 147 HMS *Broadsword*—the Royal Navy's first
all-metric warship

Crown copyright

Fig. 148 Frigates

Frigates

a General Purpose Frigate *Leander* class 1963–72/ 2,860 + tonnes/113·4 m/ST/30 k. Fifteen ships in the RN. Armed with two 115-mm guns in a twin turret, two 40-mm, two 20-mm AA guns, Seacat AA missile launcher and varied armaments, and a helicopter capable of delivering homing torpedoes. **b** Type 21 *Amazon* class 1973/3,250 tonnes full load/117 m/ COGOG/30 + k. Full gas turbine-propelled fast frigate. Armed with Exocet and Seacat AA missile launchers, one 115-mm gun, two 20-mm AA, AS homing torpedoes from helicopter, six torpedo tubes. Controllable pitch propellers.* **c** West German *Bremen* class, general-purpose 1980s/3,800 t/130 m/ CODOG/30 k. Armed with 1 dual-purpose 76 mm gun forward, 2 quadruple Harpoon long range anti-ship launchers, medium range and close-in AA launchers, 4 lightweight torpedo tubes, 2 helicopters. **d** US *Oliver Hazard Perry* class—54 ships on completion of series 1980s/3,700 t/135 m/COGOG/ 28 k. Armed with Harpoon anti-ship launchers, 1 76 mm AA gun, 20 mm AA guns, 4 torpedo tubes, 2 helicopters. Ships of same class in navies of Australia, Turkey and Spain. **e** Italian anti-submarine *Maestrale* class 1980s/3,040 t/122 m/CODOG/33 k. Armed with anti-ship missile launchers (range up to 90 miles), 1 127 mm gun forward, medium range AA launchers and 40 mm Bofors AA guns, 4 torpedo tubes, 2 helicopters. **f** General-purpose frigate *Broadsword* class (Type 22) 1978/4,000 tonnes/131 m/ COGOG/29 k. 14 vessels are planned to replace the *Leander* class. Equipped with Exocet missile systems and homing torpedoes and Seawolf anti-aircraft missiles. 2 Lynx helicopters.

The first Type 23 frigate (Duke Class), HMS *Norfolk*, incorporates many improvements resulting from RN experience in the Falklands.

---

* Two Type 21 class frigates were lost in the Falklands.

Light Escort Vessels or Corvettes

It is difficult to make a clear distinction between a destroyer and a frigate and, similarly, the dividing line between the frigate and the escort is not always clear. Many frigates have a displacement tonnage of around 2,000, but the light escort vessel is generally about half that figure. During the Second World War the corvette—based on the very seaworthy whale catcher—fulfilled the function of a light convoy escort and patrol vessel.

Fig. 149 a French Escort Vessel (*aviso*) 1970s/1250 tonnes/80 m/M/24 k. Armed with one 100-mm and two 20-mm AA guns and depth charge and torpedo AS throwers. **b** Italian *de Cristofaro* class corvette 1966/850 tonnes/80·2 m/18 k. Armed with two 76-mm guns and AS armament similar to **a**.

Submarines

The essential character of the submarine's appearance is the long, narrow hull, and the single compact superstructure. The nuclear-powered submarine has a streamlined, whale-shaped hull with a blunt nose, and the bridge is placed much further forward than on the traditional vessel. Some conventionally powered submarines have additional domelike structures on deck which house the Sonar underwater detection gear. US nuclear-powered submarines have diving planes placed horizontally on each side of the bridge—known as the sail. Conventional propulsion is by diesels, for operating at surface and periscope level, and for charging batteries ready for deep operation on electric propulsion.

Since the Second World War the submarine has developed into a formidable strategic weapon of devastating power and world-wide range. The *snort* (first used by the Germans during the war) is a breathing tube, or air mast, which projects above the bridge and enables the vessel to take in fresh air while cruising just below the surface, and to remain submerged for much longer periods. The introduction of nuclear power has meant that the vessels are true submarines—and not just submersible vessels—able to cruise for thousands of miles without refuelling and without surfacing. Continuous fresh air is obtained by circulation through a regenerative plant. The largest submarines are armed with *Polaris*, *Poseidon*, *Trident* or Russian *SS-N-20* intercontinental ballistic missiles with nuclear warheads. They are, in effect, submerged mobile platforms with weapon systems capable of destroying land targets within a range of up to 6,000 nautical miles. Also armed with standard 533-metre torpedoes, they can operate in naval actions as hunter-killer units.

Fig. 150 The submarine

sonar dome

USS b idge

diving planes

sail

forward
hydroplane

periscope,
radar and radio
standards

navigating
bridge or
conning tower

control

torpedoes

accommodation

batteries

3 sonar domes

swimmer delivery
vehicles

snort

nuclear
reactor

reactor
control

steam turbines

electric motors
(alternative power)

after hydroplane

rudders

guided missile
tubes

sonar dome

Submarines in the world's navies fall into three main categories; these can be represented by examples from the Royal Navy. **c** Nuclear-powered Ballistic Missile Submarine *Resolution* class, 1967–9/7,500 tonnes surface—8,400 tonnes submerged/129·5 m/ NST/20 k surface and 25 k submerged. Armed with Polaris surface-to-surface intercontinental missiles. Also six 533-mm torpedo homing tubes forward. Each submarine has two separate crews of 141 each in order to allow the greatest possible time at sea on very long operations. **d** Nuclear-powered Fleet Submarine *Valiant* class 1966 onwards/3,500 tonnes surface and 4,500 tonnes submerged/86·9 m and 82·9 m/NST/30 k. These ships are designed as true warships to hunt and kill enemy submarines and surface ships, and are equipped with six 533-mm torpedo tubes. **e** British *Swiftsure* class 1981 onwards/ 4,500 tonnes submerged/underwater speed 30 k. Anti-submarine torpedoes and Harpoon anti-ship missiles. Nuclear powered. The *Trafalgar* class is a further development of this class. **f** Patrol Submarine *Oberon* class 1960–7/2,030 tonnes surface and 2,410 tonnes submerged/90·0 m/M and E/12 k surface and 17 submerged. Armed with eight tubes for standard 533-mm homing torpedoes. Part of the superstructure is made of glass fibre laminate. **g** The last *Porpoise* class sub. is to become a museum vessel on the Thames Embankment. **h** US vessel with facilities for carrying amphibious warfare equipment. **i** USSR submarine *Delta* class with above deck missile tanks.

A development of **c** will be the four RN *Vanguard* class submarines armed with *Trident II* sea-launched missiles. With a displacement of 15,000 tonnes they will be about twice the size of those of the *Resolution* class.

Crown copyright

Fig. 151 HMS *Cottesmore* is one of the 1980s Hunt class Mine Countermeasures ships, built of glass reinforced plastic.

Fig. 152 'Ton' class coastal minesweeper on Fisheries Protection duties

Mine Warfare Ships

During hostilities minesweeping is often carried out by different types of vessel temporarily fitted for the purpose; many well-known paddle steamers were used in both world wars. Specially built ships are now classified into three groups: ocean, coastal and inshore. Within the general heading of mine warfare ships are *minelayers*, whose function is to lay mines in enemy waters; *minehunters*, fitted with sonar mine-hunting equipment capable of locating and classifying mines on the sea-bed from a distance; *minesweepers*, equipped with mine-destroying gear for sweeping contact mines from the surface. The *contact* mine is moored to the sea-bed and floats just below the surface of the sea, exploding on contact with a vessel. It is cleared by long sweepers which are towed on each quarter by the minesweeper, so that the mine can be cut from its mooring. The *magnetic* mine lies on the sea-bed and is activated by the proximity of a ship's steel hull. It must be discovered and detonated by electrical means at a safe distance. The *acoustic* mine also lies on the sea-bed and is activated by the vibrations of a nearby ship's propeller or engines; it must be destroyed by acoustical means. For obvious reasons the minesweeper must have as small a magnetic field as possible; for this reason the smaller vessels have wooden hulls and a good deal of aluminium in their structure. Some ships even have non-magnetic engines, and in recent years fibre-glass and reinforced plastic have been used. The latest ships are equipped with electronic methods of mine detection and destruction.

Mine Warfare Ships

Fig. 153 Mine warfare ships

Fig. 154 Swedish minelayer cum depot ship. *Älvsborg*

By courtesy of the Swedish Naval Attaché

a Swedish Minelayer and Submarine Depot Ship *Älvsborg* class 1971/2,650 tonnes/92·4 m/M/15 k. A dual-purpose vessel with accommodation for 200 men in addition to the crew. On the stern ramp are several minelaying rails running parallel over the low counter. **b** British Mine Countermeasure support ship and minelayer HMS *Abdiel* 1967. Paid off in 1988, to be converted to a commercial car ferry. **c** British 'Ton' class coastal minesweeper and minehunter. 1953–60/425 tonnes/46·6 m/M/15 k. Also employed in Fishery Protection and headquarters for each of eleven units of the Royal Naval Reserve. Hulls of mahogany, aluminium or glass fibre to reduce magnetic attraction. 'Hunt' class to be improved version. **d** British Hunt class minehunter 1979 onwards/675 t/60 m/15 k armed with 1 Bofors AA gun. Hulls of reinforced plastic. **e** French *Circe* class minehunters 1971–3/460 tonnes/46·3 m/M/15 k. The French Navy also has a large number of ocean and coastal minesweepers similar to the British 'Ton' class and some ex-United States classes. **f** Danish Minelayer *Falster* class 1963–4/1,900 tonnes/77 m/M/17 k. Strengthened for ice navigation, she is equipped with two twin mountings of 76-mm guns.

Depot Ships

In appearance, the naval depot ship resembles a large merchantman with high topsides, many portholes and a number of heavy derricks or deck cranes, except that she is painted grey. Her function is to serve as a 'mother' ship to a group of particular warships such as submarines, destroyers or coastal craft. The depot ship is well equipped with workshops and all the materials required for servicing the relevant warships. In addition she may have accommodation, catering and recreational facilities, a chapel, hospital with operating theatre, and a dental surgery. In the US Navy the term 'tender' is used. In recent years tenders for nuclear-powered fleet ballistic missile submarines have been familiar at the US base in the Holy Loch in Scotland.

---

a USS *Emory S.Land* class submarine maintenance support ship. 23,000 tonnes/197 m/ST/18 k. Floating base for 12 nuclear powered submarines. **b** US Navy *Yellowstone* class tender for destroyers. 20,500 tonnes/ 196 m/ST/18 k. **c** USS *Canopus* 1964/21,450 tonnes/ 196·0 m/ST/18 k. Fleet Ballistic Missile Submarine tender. Facilities for accommodating three submarines at any one time. **d** USSR *Ugra* class nuclear submarine support ship 1961 + /9,000 tonnes/141 m/ M/17. Heavier armament than is usual for a depot ship—eight 57-mm guns in twin mounts. **e** Australian Destroyer Tender *Stalwart* 1968/10,000 tonnes/ 157·1 m/M/20 k.

a

b

c helideck

d

e helideck

Fig. 155 Depot ships

153

Patrol Boats

The main characteristics of the fast patrol boat are its small size and its great speed, the latter often in the region of 40 knots. Three main types of craft are built; the *gunboat* armed with a single or twin 40-mm Bofors gun, the *guided missile boat* armed with surface-to-surface missile launchers, and the *torpedo boat* with two or four single 533-mm torpedo tubes. Sometimes craft are designed to be interchangeable, i.e. torpedo or gunboats. The British firm of Vosper Thornycroft, of Southampton, has specialized in the design and construction of fast patrol boats and many of the world's navies possess boats from its yards.

Fig. 156   Malaysian fast patrol boat 1960s/96 tonnes/ 31·39 m/M/27 k. Vosper Thornycroft

The US Navy possesses several classes of 40-knot boats (some of them propelled by CODOG systems and armed with missile launchers) and a number of hydrofoil boats with a new type of gas turbine propulsion in which the propeller is replaced by rearward water jets. The Russian missile boats are capable of firing surface-to-surface missiles with a range of 18 miles. The hoods over the launchers are distinctive features (**Fig. 156b**). The much slower RN *Castle*, *Peacock* and *Island* class vessels are designed for fishery and oil installation protection and general offshore duties.

Fig. 157 HMS *Hecla* class 1965–6/
2,733 gt/79·3 m/DE/14 k maximum

Survey Ships

For many years the Admiralty has been responsible
for the production of world-wide navigation charts
and sailing directions. For this purpose the Royal
Navy—and similarly other navies—operates a number of specially designed survey ships. In the past
some of the ships had other functions as well, but the
latest examples are used solely for oceanographical
and hydrographical work. The survey ship must
have a long cruising range and be strengthened
against ice. **Fig. 157** shows a class of British survey
ship which is very well equipped with drawing
offices, chart room, laboratories, workshops, library,
cinema and hospital. She also, like so many contemporary warships and auxiliaries, has a helicopter
landing deck.

The latest United States survey ships are similar
vessels with a distinctive motor yacht appearance.
They have an extensive cruising range of between
10,000 and 15,000 nautical miles, and in order to
increase their manoeuvrability they are fitted with a
bow thruster unit and controllable pitch propeller.
The newest French survey ship has a rather different
appearance from those described above as she has a
slightly boxlike general appearance, and the superstructure three-quarters aft.

Fig. 158   Space event ship: *Komarov*
USSR/1968/8,900 gt/155·6 m/M/22 k

The French guided missile destroyer illustrated on page 136 has one prominent radar dome. The most unusual vessel with three huge domes, shown here in profile, is one of two similar ships designed to work in connection with spacecraft. Another vessel for the same purpose, although considerably larger, is named after the Russian cosmonaut Gagarin. She has four large radar dishes instead of domes, a massive navigating bridge and funnel with super-structure aft.

Fig. 159   Mooring salvage
and boom vessel

boom gallows
and sheaves

This specialized type of auxiliary is required for the handling of heavy moorings and for maintaining the net booms and gates provided in wartime for the protection of warships against torpedo attack. The easily recognized feature is the pair of horns projecting over the bows to which the moorings or buoys can be lifted. The late 1980s RMAS *Sal* ... vessels, 2,000 gt and length 77 metres, have a powerful crane on the foredeck capable of a 400-tonne lift and a bow lift of half that amount. They are also equipped for fire fighting and dealing with pollution control.

Fleet Auxiliaries

Ships of the Royal Fleet Auxiliary Service (RFA) play an important role in maintaining the efficiency of fighting ships in peace and in war; they carry oil, fuel, dry cargo, spare parts and many thousands of miscellaneous, but essential, items. They are fitted with varied specialized equipment for supplying RN ships in harbour and at sea, well away from their home ports. In general the ships are similar in appearance to commercial cargo carriers with cargo-handling gear, but much more deck clutter, and they are manned by officers and ratings of the Merchant Navy. Recently helicopters have made a very useful contribution to the work of these support ships and most of the latter now have a helideck aft; some have a helicopter hangar as well.

Operation of the helicopters is in the hands of RN officers and ratings. With the exception of a few tankers, ships of the RFA are painted grey overall, with a light grey funnel and a black top. The ships wear the Blue Ensign defaced by a golden anchor (**Fig. 110**). The procedure of replenishing warships at sea requires fast and easily manoeuvrable servicing vessels. The latter take up a position on a steady course parallel to, and about 35 metres from the receiving warship and proceed at exactly the same speed. In order to reduce motion, they both steam into the wind, or against the sea, whichever is the stronger. After contact is made by firing a nylon line across the gap, the oil hoses or jackstays can be sent across and the oil or stores transferred, while the two ships keep up the same speed and course (page 112).

Logistics Landing Ship

Fig. 160 RFA *Sir Geraint* 1970/5,674 tonnes/125·6 m/ M/17 k. Reference has been made on pages 56–62 to RO/RO passenger and cargo vessels, and the drawing below shows a military version of this type of ship. One of several such vessels, she is designed to carry over 300 soldiers and their vehicles for combined services landing operations. With the bow ramp and door she is a development of the wartime tank landing craft, but in addition there are drive-through facilities with a stern door and vehicle ramp. Access from one deck to another is by ramps. The vessel is

bow ramp · 3-tonne cranes · daytime landing deck · 20-tonne cranes · helicopter landing deck · stern ramp

equipped with workshops for repair and maintenance of military vehicles. The helicopter landing deck aft of the superstructure can be used at all times during daylight; in calm weather, helicopters can also be landed on the deck amidships, when the deck cranes can be swung out of the way. Armament consists only of a pair of 40-mm Bofors guns for AA defence. Similar ships of a new series have better facilities for loading helicopters on the foredeck. *Sir Galahad* was lost in the Falklands and *Sir Tristram*, badly damaged, was brought home on board a semi-submersible heavy lift ship (page 32).

Fig. 161 *Arromanches* class 1981/282 tonnes/ 33 m/9 k

Landing Craft (Operated by the army Royal Corps of Transport)

The logistics landing craft described opposite is designed so that army vehicles can be driven direct from the ship to the beach during a combined forces operation. Any such operation would also need a number of smaller craft, with bow doors, for the same purpose as in the 'D'-Day landings on the north coast of France in June 1944. Earlier in the war this type of landing craft developed from the broad-beamed barge and became a large open-decked vessel with shallow draught and a hinged ramp in the square bows.

Some vessels are as long as 70 metres and carry a large number of troops and vehicles, but the craft built to be carried by assault ships are 24-m vessels with the same characteristics. These new vessels are very seaworthy and are fitted with Kort nozzle rudders (page 16) to ensure better steering and control in shallow waters close to a beach. They are referred to as LCM or Landing Craft Mechanized, as they are capable of transporting either two battle tanks or about 100 tonnes of army vehicles. Some smaller craft in the US Navy are LCVP or Landing Craft Vehicle and Personnel, and experiments are now being made with 30-m air-cushion landing craft with gas turbines and aircraft-type propellers giving a speed of 50 knots. The larger craft are usually conveyed to the scene of amphibious operations in the wet dock of assault ships (page 135) and the smaller as deck cargo.

HD = helicopter deck
G = goalpost masts

lifeboats

hanger 'HD

funnel uptakes on
starboard side

113 m flight deck

Fig. 162 Royal Fleet Auxiliaries

Royal Fleet Auxiliaries

a Replenishment ship *Regent* class 1967/22,890 tonnes/195·1 m/ST/20 k. Complement composed of 119 RFA crew, 52 civil servants and 11 RN officers and ratings for flying and maintaining the helicopter. The long high poop, with landing deck and hangar, distinguishes the profile from that of a freighter. This is a new purpose-built ship designed to carry dry cargo and ammunition for transfer at sea. **b** Fleet Replenishment Oiler '*Ol*' class 1965/36,000 tonnes/197·5 m/ST/19 k. This type of supply ship is distinguished from the commercial tanker by the helideck and the number of heavy goalposts with their jackstays and hose-handling gear. Ships in this class are strengthened against ice; *Olna* has a bow thruster unit. **c** *Rover* class oiler 1970–11,522 tonnes/140·3 m/M/19 k. A smaller type of oiler than **b**, but designed also to transfer oil fuel, fresh water, dry cargo or stores underway either by helicopter or by the method outlined on page 157. **d** Helicopter Support Ship *Engadine* 1967. Future uncertain but role to be undertaken by RFA *Argus*. **e** RFA *Fort Grange* 1978/17,000 gt/183 m/20 k. 4 Sea King helicopters. Carries all types of naval stores and ammunition. **f** RFA *Argus* 1987/28,081 t/175 m/19 k. Classed as an Air Training Ship and designed to replace RFA *Engadine*, this vessel is a converted RO/RO container freighter. Carries six Sea King helicopters and can transport, and fly-off, twelve VTOL Sea Harriers. RFA *Diligence* (1981) is a Fleet Maintenance Unit with an unusual silhouette—the super-structure is well forward and is surmounted by a large helideck.

Traditionally RFAs have been classed as unarmed merchant ships but, increasingly they are being equipped with light defence weapons.

Fig. 163 The Royal Yacht *Britannia*

The royal yacht *Britannia* was built by John Brown Ltd of Clydebank and was accepted by the Admiralty in January 1954, nine months after she had been launched by Her Majesty the Queen.

The *Britannia* was designed as a dual-purpose vessel: for the peace-time role of conveying members of the royal family to any part of the globe and for the wartime role of naval hospital ship when her stabilizers, special air-conditioning and large laundry would be of special importance. She has two sets of turbines modelled on those made for fast cross-Channel packets giving her a continuous sea speed of 21 knots. She has a gross tonnage of 5,769 and an overall length of 125·5 m. Special attention has been given to the design of the funnel to ensure the minimum interference from smoke and waste gases; the funnel and superstructure above the bridge deck are constructed of aluminium alloy.

The *Britannia*'s royal apartments are placed aft between the main and mizzen masts. Custom demands three masts as when the Sovereign is on board the following flags must be worn: Royal Standard at the main, Lord High Admiral's flag at the fore and Union Flag at the mizzen. The White Ensign is always flown at the stern.

Battleship

In 1906 the all-big-gun turbine-driven HMS *Dreadnought* revolutionised battleship design and set the pattern for the most important and most powerful unit of the world's navies. For nearly half a century the heavily armed, and armoured, battleship and the slightly faster battle-cruiser, dominated sea power. In 1914 Britain alone had 75 warships of these two types and this number had dropped to 15 by 1939. During the 1939–45 war the activities, and tragic losses, of ships such as HMS *Hood, Royal Oak, Repulse, Prince of Wales*, the German *Bismarck* and *Tirpitz*, and the Japanese *Yamato* (the largest of them all), are well known and their names will always be remembered. After the war it was evident that the development of the aircraft carrier, with its very effective striking power, had made the battleship too vulnerable to air attack and it was therefore obsolete. However, in spite of this, 40 years later, 4 American *Iowa* class battleships have been brought out of mothballing and refitted with the latest electronic surveillance and control systems, several guided missile weapons systems, and 4 helicopters. Their triple-turret 16 in. (406 mm) guns have been retained for long-range shore bombardment as they were so used during the Vietnam war.

Fig. 164
USS *New Jersey* operating as a fire support ship off Vietnam in 1969

Official US Navy photograph

Fig. 165
French
frigate
*By courtesy of
French Naval
Attaché*

Fig. 166 Swedish fast patrol boat armed with one
57-mm gun, light missiles and six torpedo tubes
By courtesy of Swedish Naval Attaché

Fig. 167 RFA *Bayleaf* (1982), ex-merchant ship
By courtesy of Jim Prentice

UNITED STATES CLASSIFICATION OF NAVAL SHIPS AND SERVICE CRAFT

Aircraft Carriers: Attack carrier **CVA**; Nuclear Attack carrier **CVAN**; Support carrier **CVS**. *Surface Combatants:* Battleship **BB**; Heavy cruiser **CA**; Guided missile cruiser **CG**; Nuclear guided missile cruiser **CGN**; Light cruiser **CL**; Guided missile light cruiser **CLG**; Destroyer **DD**; Guided missile Destroyer **DDG**; Radar picket destroyer **DDR**; Frigate **DL**; Guided missile frigate **DLG**; Nuclear missile frigate **DLGN**. *Ocean Escorts:* Escort ship **DE**; Guided missile escort ship **DEG**; Radar picket escort ship **DER**. *Command ship* **CC**. *Submarines* **SS**; Nuclear submarine **SSN**; Guided missile submarine **SSG**; Fleet ballistic missile submarine (nuclear) **SSBN**. *Patrol ships* **P**. *Amphibious Warfare Ships:* (selection) Command ship **LCC**; Fire support ship **LFS**; Assault ship **LPH**; Amphibious transport submarine **LPSS**; Dock landing ship **LSD**; Tank landing ship **LST**. *Mine Warfare Ships:* Countermeasure ship **MCS**; Coastal minesweeper (non-magnetic) **MSC**; Fleet minesweeper (steel hull) **MSF**; Ocean minesweeper (non-magnetic) **MSO**. *Combatant Craft:* Patrol craft (hydrofoil) **PCH**; Patrol gunboat (hydrofoil) **PGH**; Fast patrol craft **PTF**. *Landing Craft:* Assault **LCA**; Mechanized **LCM**; Personnel (large) **LCPL**; Personnel (ramped) **LCPR**; Utility **LCU**; Vehicle (personnel) **LCVP**; Warping tug **LWT**. *Mines Counter-measures Craft:* Boat **MSB**; Drone **MSD**; Inshore **MSI**; Launch **MSL**; River **MSM**; Patrol **MSR**; Special (device) **MSS**. *Riverine warfare craft:* various with no common letter. *Auxiliaries* **A**. *Service craft* code begins with **A** or **Y**.

American warships show hull numbers but not type designation letters (cf. page 120).

Fig. 168 Parts of a sailing vessel

truck

main gaff topsail

main topmast staysail

mainmast

foremast

fore upper tops'l

fore lower tops'l

flying jib

outer jib

jib

fore staysail

bobstay

ou er bobstay

spike bowsprit

crew

hold

shrouds

companion

skylight

cabin

wheel

boom

mainsail

foresail

166

7 SAILING SHIPS

PARTS OF A SAILING SHIP
(TOPSAIL SCHOONER)

Rigging

A	Jib and forestaysail sheets
B	Upper and lower topsail braces
C	Fore braces
D	Fore sheet
E	Main peak halliards (or halyards)
F	Fore peak halliards
G	Main sheet
H	Main boom topping lift
I	Forestay
J	Fore topmast backstay
K	Main topmast backstay
L	Signal halliards
RP	Reef points

Rigging can be divided into two categories: *standing rigging*, which helps to maintain masts in their permanent positions, and *running rigging*, which controls the movement of yards and sails.

Standing Rigging

A forestay passes from the top of a mast downwards in a forward direction.

A backstay passes from the top of a mast downwards to both sides of the vessel to take the forward strain of the mast.

Shrouds pass from the top of a mast (or a point on it) to the ship's sides.

Ratlines are short lengths of line which cross the shrouds at intervals and form ladders to the upper parts of the masts.

Running Rigging

A lift takes the weight of a yard or boom.

Halliards raise or lower a spar or sail, or may be used for signal flags.

Braces control the fore-and-aft movement of the yards.

Clew lines lift the lower corners of a square sail.

To *bend* a sail is to attach it to a yard or boom, and to *furl* it is to secure it temporarily to a spar by short lengths of line called gaskets. The spike bowsprit has generally taken the place of the more elaborate jib-boom bowsprit. The former consists of one spar only.

The names of the spars, sails and rigging of a large square-rigged vessel follow the same system of nomenclature as shown for the topsail schooner.

These are the names of the sails of a square-rigged mast, starting from deck level: *course, lower-topsail, upper-topsail, lower-topgallant, upper-topgallant, royal* and in some instances *skysail*. Names of masts of a four-mast barque: *fore, main, mizzen* and *jigger*.

In naming a sail the name of the mast comes first, followed by the name of the sail. For example: *fore upper-topsail* refers to the third sail from deck level on the foremast, and *mizzen upper-topgallant* refers to the fifth sail on the third mast of a full-rigged ship or four-masted barque.

The *mizzen-course* is sometimes referred to as the *cro'jack*. Several giant five-mast barques have been built and their fifth masts have been variously called *after-jigger, after spanker* or *pusher*.

At the present time serious studies are being made for the possible re-introduction of the large cargo-carrying sailing ship on grounds of economy. Some of these are based on the traditional square sail, but controlled mechanically by computer, while others are concerned with a new type of aerofoil sail on un-stayed masts.

Sailing Schoolships

Before the last war a few square-rigged ocean-going ships were employed in the carriage of cargoes, mainly in the Australian grain trade. In the post-war period the German cargo-cadet four-masted barques *Pamir* and *Passat* sailed in this trade, but after the former foundered in a hurricane off the Azores in September 1957, with the loss of 80 lives, the other vessel was laid up. Interest in sail was revived in 1956 with the first of the 'Tall Ships' races from Torbay to Lisbon, established by the Sail Training Association. The opportunity of seeing so many square-rigged and other large sailing vessels together created great excitement, and this has been maintained by the biennial race held on different courses.

Enthusiasts in this country alone have always regretted that Great Britain, almost alone of the seafaring nations, has not possessed a square-rigged sailing schoolship. This is now being rectified by the building of the barque *Lord Nelson* by the Jubilee Sailing Trust, for the physically handicapped. Some governments provide, by means of their sailing schoolships, long courses of professional training for boys who wish to take up a career at sea either in the merchant navy or in fighting ships. Most of the sailing schoolships provide shorter courses for boys—or girls—as a part of general education, in the belief that qualities of leadership and the development of character can result. There are about 30 square-rigged sailing schoolships in service and many more fore-and-aft rigged craft serving the same purpose. About 30 more ships and barques are employed as floating schools, or museums. A few of these vessels were originally cargo-carriers built towards the end of the nineteenth century.

Full-rigged Ship

The **full-rigged ship** is a sailing vessel with square sails on all three, or four, masts. This was the rig of many of the fine sailing vessels of the middle nineteenth century when the famous China tea clippers achieved such high speeds and performance. The British ship, *Cutty Sark*, was the most famous of these. Built at Dumbarton in 1869 with a tonnage of 921 gt, and a length of 64·61 m, she made many record passages. After a period as a stationary sail training ship, she is now restored and dry-berthed at Greenwich. The Glasgow-built ship *Balclutha* (1886) has also been restored and remains afloat at the San Francisco Maritime Museum.

Fig. 169
Full-rigged ship

Ship-rigged Schoolships

Owned by the town of Kristiansand, the Norwegian *Sørlandet* was built in 1927 with a tonnage of 577 gross and an overall length of 32·42 m. She has accommodation for about 100 cadets. During the last war she was almost completely destroyed. In 1947 she was entirely rebuilt along with the *Christian Radich*, which had capsized during the war and also

Fig. 170
Danish
Schoolship
Full-rigged
ship *Danmark*

*Skyfotos,
Ashford, Kent*

seemed to be beyond repair. Built in 1937, she is a slightly larger vessel of 676 tons gross and a length of 58·52 m, and has accommodation for about the same number of cadets. She is based on Oslo. The Danish *Danmark* of 1933 has a tonnage of 777 tons gross, a length of 57·29 m and can carry rather more cadets than the two Norwegian ships. The *Georg Stage*, also belonging to Denmark, was built in 1935 to replace a ship of the same name which became the *Joseph Conrad* and was run for several years as a privately owned schoolship. The latter is now preserved at Mystic, Connecticut. The present ship—203 tons, 37·48 m can be identified by her black hull. Poland now has a new full-rigged sail training ship, *Dar Mlodziezy* built in 1981, to replace the ex-cargo carrier *Dar Pomorza* of 1909. The Italian *Amerigo Vespucci* (1930) is an unusual looking ship with a very high freeboard and hull which is reminiscent of the early nineteenth-century ships-of-the-line. Argentina's *Libertad* (1962) has a gross tonnage of 3,765 and a full complement of 360 officers, crew and cadets. Another very fine full-rigged ship is the *Mir* of the USSR built in 1987 with a length of 110 m o.a. and accommodation for 100 crew and cadets.

Fig. 171 Three-masted barque

Barque

By the end of the nineteenth century the **barque**
rig had beome popular. It differed from the ship rig
in that no square sails were crossed on the mizzen
and consequently a smaller crew was required. At
this time there was a shortage of crews and many
full-rigged ships were converted to barque rig; it was
found that they often gained in sailing qualities. In
the first decades of this century the sailing ship
rapidly declined in numbers. Between the wars a
shipowner from the Baltic Åland Islands bought a
number of the barques and operated them in the
Australian grain trade—undermanned and unin-
sured. Some of these merchant vessels carried cadets,
but they were not sail training ships in the true sense.

Barque-rigged Schoolships

One of the most modern craft of this rig is the West
German *Gorch Fock* of 1,870 tonnes displacement,
built in 1959 to carry 140 cadets. She has a long poop
and the characteristic German double spanker gaffs
instead of the normal single spanker. The Norwegian
1,710 tonne barque *Statsraad Lehmkuhl*, built in 1914
as the *Grossherzog Friedrich August*, is based at
Bergen. Perhaps the best known of all the sail training

vessels is the American *Eagle* built in Germany in 1936 as the *Horst Wessel*, 1,600 tonnes displacement, and a length of 80 m, taken over at the end of the war by the US Coast Guard Service. One of her sisterships, *Gorch Fock*, passed to Russia to be renamed *Tovarisch* while yet another sister, *Albert Leo Schlageter* now sails as the Portuguese *Sagres* II. Russia's huge *Krusenstern* and *Sedov* are both ex-cargo carrying four-masted barques. Other four-masters are the new Japanese *Nippon Maru* II (1984) built to replace the earlier vessel of the same name and her sistership *Kaiwo Maru* (1930).

Some other active three-masted barques
Mircea (1938) Romania; *Gloria* (1968) Colombia; *Guayas* (1977) Ecuador; *Cuauhtemoc* (1981) Mexico; *Simon Bolivar* (1980) Venuzuela.

Floating museum ships occasionally going to sea
Nippon Maru (1930) Yokohama; *Star of India* (1863) San Diego; *Elissa* (1877) Galveston.

Fig. 172   Italian schoolship *Amerigo Vespucci*

173

Brig

The **brig** is a two-mast sailing vessel with square sails on each mast and fore-and-aft staysails, jibs and a spanker. This was a common rig for coastal and short-sea traders of the last century, and the well-known East-coast colliers were usually rigged in this way. Some of the fastest brigs of the period were the fish carriers, bringing cod from the Newfoundland Banks to Bristol and other ports. The **snow** was

Fig. 173   Brig

similar to the brig except that the spanker was set on a trysail-mast just abaft the main lower mast, which extended from the deck to the main top. Later the term referred to either a snow, or brig rigged vessel from the Baltic. During the nineteenth century the Royal Navy continued to use both brigs and snows as training ships long after steamships had become firmly established in the fleet.

The brig *Royalist* was launched in 1971. Owned by the Navy League, she is operated by the Sea Cadet Corps from her base in Portsmouth Harbour. Her 'period' look with painted square ports and stern boat davits ensures that she is easily identified.

Fig. 174
British Schoolship.
Brig *Royalist*
Skyfotos, Ashford, Kent

Brigantine

The **brigantine** has two masts, the foremast fully square-rigged and the mainmast with gaff mainsail and staysails. This rig was earlier known as the **hermaphrodite** *brig*, as the real brig had square topsails on the main topmast, but the term soon dropped out of use. The brigantine rigged schoolship *Wilhelm Pieck* was built in 1951 for the training of merchant seamen in Eastern Germany. The Irish *Asgard II* and the New Zealand *Breeze* were built in 1981.

Fig. 175
Brigantine similar to the '*Eye of the wind*' on world-wide adventure and exploration voyages for young people

Barquentine

The **barquentine** is a three-mast vessel with square sails on the foremast, staysails between the fore and main masts, and gaff sails and gaff topsails on the main and mizzen masts. This type evolved in order to reduce running costs; fore and aft sails require less manpower than square sails. The schoolship *Mercator*, owned by the Belgian government, is a good example of the barquentine. Built at Leith in 1932; she is now a museum ship at Ostend. The Indonesian *Dewarutji* is a similar vessel built in Germany in 1952 to accommodate 78 cadets and a crew of 32. Some other examples of this rig are the Swedish *Amorina* (1934); the American *Regina Maris* (1908) and the two Polish training vessels *Pogoria* (1980) and *Iskra*

Fig. 176
Barquentine

(1982). A former Portuguese Grand Banks fishing vessel, the barquentine *Gazela of Philadelphia* is now preserved in Philadelphia, USA. Also built for the Newfoundland fisheries was the steel barquentine *Palinuro* (1934) now employed by the Italian Navy in sea-training for lower-deck ratings.

Fig. 177
Juan Sebastian de Elcano

Topsail schooner

The **topsail schooner** is a fore-and-aft rigged sailing vessel with one or more square sails set on the foremast; it is the commonest rig of the smaller present-day schoolship. The largest likely to be seen in European waters is the Spanish *Juan Sebastian de Elcano*, launched in Spain in 1927 (designed in Great Britain), with a length of 93·83 m and a displacement tonnage of 3,222. She has a long poop, several deckhouses, boats and other gear between the forecastle and poop. Her near sister, but barquentine-rigged ship, built about the same time, became the Chilean *Esmeralda*, which normally operates in the Pacific.

The British Sail Training Association's pair of elegant two-masted topsail schooners *Malcolm Miller* and *Sir Winston Churchill* can accommodate 34 boys, or girls, and 9 men. Based on Portsmouth, they undertake fortnightly training cruises and also take part in the biennial Tall Ships Race. Another British ship, built in 1971, the *Captain Scott*, took part in similar cruises based on the west coast of Scotland. After only 7 years there she was sold to Oman and, as *Shabab Oman (Youth of Oman)*, pursues the same activity for young people. Two pairs of tops'l schooners are now familiar in European waters. The French Government two-mast tops'l schooners *La*

Fig. 178
Sir Winston Churchill

Belle-Poule and *L'Etoile*, built in 1932, cross two yards on the foremast with roller reefing gear for the topsail. They are modelled on the small Breton schooners or *terre neuvas* of the Newfoundland cod fisheries. The two Swedish schooners, *Gladan* and *Falken*, are 214-ton vessels built in 1947. They can be differentiated from the French pair by their single yards and running square sail, as well as the gaff fore topsail in place of the French vessels' main topmast staysail.

An increasing number of schooners—and a few square-riggers—are being used to carry passengers on holiday cruises. The most important areas for this new activity are the Maine coast of USA and the Carribean. Two of the largest schooners—both gaff rigged—are the *Fantome*, built in 1929 as a luxury yacht, now carrying over 100 passengers and the *Flying Cloud* of 1935 carrying about 80 passengers.

For many years Lord Runciman's famous yacht the three-mast topsail schooner *Sunbeam II* was well known in her original role, and later as the Swedish sail training vessel *Flying Clipper*. This schooner is now the Greek *Eugene Eugenides*.

In the last century, but in rapidly diminishing numbers during this one, the trading schooner was very common around British shores. No vessel now exists in trade but, fortunately, two of the last vessels have been preserved. The Maritime Trust has the last British wooden trading schooner, *Kathleen and May* (1900), now preserved in St Katherine's Dock, London. The last actual trading schooner *Result* (1893)—in her last days reduced to a two-mast auxiliary sailing vessel—had been acquired for preservation by the Ulster Folk and Transport Museum near Belfast.

Fig. 179
*Kathleen
and May*
(1900)

Fig. 180
Result:
original rig
of 1893

Labels on figure: topmast, topsail, sprit, mainsail, brails, mizzen, flying jib, staysail, foresail, bowsprit, lee-board

Fig. 181
Thames spritsail barge

Sailing Barge

In the early part of this century about 2,000 sailing barges traded in the Thames estuary and along the South and East coasts, and this number has now dwindled away to one or two barges trading, or on charter. Interest in this attractive survival of sail is, however, retained when most of the 20 or so survivors—mainly as private yachts—take part in the Pin Mill, Blackwater and Medway annual sailing barge races.

The characteristic feature of the barge is the huge mainsail supported by a 15–18 metre sprit. For furling, this sail is gathered up to the mast by means of brails. This feature, and others, enable the craft to be sailed by only two men. Not all barges have a bowsprit and some have a gaff and boom 'mule rigged' mizzen. Both masts are set in tabernacles so that they can be lowered for the negotiation of low bridges. The sailing barge *Cambria* (built at Greenhithe in 1905) is now preserved in St. Katherine's Dock, London.

8 GENERAL INFORMATION Part II

Abbreviations

A foremost gun turret; **AA** anti-aircraft; **AS** anti-submarine; **ASDIC** Allied Submarine Detection Investigation Committee; **B** second gun turret from bows; **bhp** brake horse power; **bp** between perpendiculars; **CODOG** combined diesel/gas turbine propulsion; **COGOG** full gas turbine propulsion; **COSAG** combined steam/gas turbines; **CSD** closed shelter deck; **DE** diesel-electric; **DF** direction finder; **DP** dual-purpose; **d.w.** or **dwt** deadweight tonnage; **FAA** Fleet Air Arm; **FPB** fast patrol boat; **FV** fishing vessel; **GP** general purpose; **gt** or **g.r.t.** gross registered tonnage; **GT** gas turbine; **HA/LA** high angle/low angle; **HMAS** Her Majesty's Australian Ship; **HMNZS** Her Majesty's New Zealand Ship; **HMS** Her Majesty's Ship; **HWOST** high water ordinary spring tides; **k** knot; **LASH** Lighter aboard ship vessel; **LPG** liquefied propane gas carrier; **LR** Lloyd's Register; **LWOST** low water ordinary spring tides; **MN** Merchant Navy; **MTB** motor torpedo boat; **MV** merchant ship or motor vessel; **NAC** Naval Air Command; **n.r.t.** net registered tonnage; **o.a.** length overall; **OBO** oil/bulk/ore carrier; **OSD** open shelter deck; **PS** paddle steamer; **RFA** Royal Fleet Auxiliary; **RM** Royal Marines; **RMAS** Royal Maritime Auxiliary Service; **RMS** Royal Mail Ship; **RN** Royal Navy; **RNLI** Royal National Lifeboat Institution; **RNR** Royal Naval Reserve; **RO/RO** roll on/roll off; **s.h.p** shaft horse power; **SOS** radiotelegraph distress signal; **SR** steam reciprocating engines; **TE** turbo electric; **SS** steamship; **TSS** turbine steamship; **USS** United States Ship; **VLCC** very large crude oil carrier; **wl** water-line; **WT** wireless telegraphy; **X** gun turret forward of the aftermost one; **Y** aftermost gun turret.

Buoyage *International Association of Lighthouse Authorities (IALA) System.* Since 1977 a new international system of buoyage has been gradually replacing about thirty systems previously in use over the world. Under the IALA scheme Europe, Africa, India, Australia and most of Asia will be under the 'A' version and North, Central and South America and parts of Asia will be under the 'B' version. The drawings show the essential features of the 'A' version—port (red) and starboard (green) referring to the left and right hand on *entering* a port, channel or estuary. Black and yellow cardinal marks, with distinctive triangular topmarks, indicate the safe water to the north, south, east or west of the submerged rocks, end of a shoal or similar danger point. A submerged wreck, isolated rock, or similar hazard with clear water all round is now indicated by a red and black mark while the Safe Water Marks indicate a mid-channel passage or landfall.

Fig. 182 IALA Buoyage System

Anchor or riding lights. An all-round white light on the forestay 6 to 12 metres above the hull and, at the stern, a similar white light 4·5 metres lower than the forward light.

on the port beam white·red·white

on the starboard beam: white·green·white

from starboard bow   right ahead   on the port bow

Steaming lights. A white light on the foremast 6 to 12 metres above the hull visible ahead and two points ($22\frac{1}{2}°$) abaft either beam; a similar white light on the mainmast at least 4·5 metres higher than the forward light. *Side or bow lights,* placed lower than the white lights and visible right ahead and two points abaft the beam, *red* on the *port* side and *green* on the *starboard* side. A white *stern light* is shown by a vessel when being overtaken.

Fig. 183 Navigation Lights for vessels over 45 metres in length

Glossary

Armour belt Band of protective steel plating on sides of a warship's water-line. **Ballast** Heavy material carried to ensure stability—usually water. **In Ballast** Sailing without cargo. **Berth** Loading or discharging position at a quay. **Bilge keel** Longitudinal external keel at turn of the hull to resist rolling and improve steering. **Binnacle** Free-standing mounting for compass. **Bitts** Pair of strong steel columns for mooring ropes. **Bollard** Single steel post on ship or quayside for mooring ropes. **Boot-topping** Area of a ship's hull roughly between the light and loaded water-lines painted a distinctive colour. **Bow thruster** Small propeller in an athwartships tunnel near a ship's stem to increase manoeuvrability at slow speeds. **Bridge deck** Superstructure containing navigating bridge, wheelhouse, chart room and captain's quarters. **Bulbous bow** Rounded projection of the ship's forefoot to reduce resistance when in ballast. **Bulkhead** Vertical transverse or longitudinal steel partition in a ship's hull. **Bulwark** 1-metre high steel plating along the side of the deck for safety of crew or passengers. **Bunker** Space for storing fuel. **Bunkers** The fuel itself. **Capstan** Upright revolving pillar for manipulating mooring or other ropes. **Catwalk** Light connecting bridge. **Coaming** Raised lip of plating round the edge of a hatchway. **Cofferdam** Double watertight bulkheads. **Companion** Ladder or staircase connecting two decks. **Conning tower** Part of a warship's bridge and the superstructure of a submarine. **Cowl** Upper part of a ventilator or smoke baffle on a funnel. **Cross-trees** Small platform at the head of a lower mast. **Davit** Radial, quadrant or gravity type fitting for support and lowering of lifeboats. **Deadlight** Watertight steel shutter to protect scuttle or porthole. **Derrick** Swinging spar for lifting and slewing cargo. **Draught**

Depth of water necessary to float a ship. **Entrance** Tapering part of hull between parallel sides and pointed stem. **Fairlead** Short vertical deck fittings for guidance of ropes. **Fender** Rope, rubber or cane pad to protect ship's side. **Flotsam** Floating goods lost by shipwreck or thrown overboard. **Forecastle** or **Fo'c'sle** Raised forward part of a ship's hull. **Freeboard** Distance between water-line and main deck. **Freighter** American term for a cargo ship. **Gaff** Spar at head of a fore-and-aft sail or similar diagonal spar for flags. **Galley** Ship's kitchen. **Gallows** Inverted U-shaped fitting at side of a fishing boat's deck. **Guided missile** Rocket type weapon. **Gunhouse** Lightly protected house on gun mounting. **Gunshield** Frontal protection for gun crew. **Gunwale** Upper edge of a boat's side. **Hance** or **fishplate** Curved plating between change of level of ship's bulwarks. **Hatchway** Opening in a deck with a movable cover, i.e. a **hatch**. **Hawespipe** Steel tube between forecastle deck and ship's side through which anchor cable passes. **Helideck** Landing platform for helicopter. **Helm** Mechanism for operating ship or boat's rudder. **Hogging** Strain on a vessel's hull when, with the crest of a wave amidships, the ends tend to droop. **Island** Raised part of ship's hull. **Jetsam** Goods thrown overboard to lighten ship and washed up ashore. **Keel** Centre longitudinal box girder forming vessel's backbone. **Keelson** or **kelson** Fore-and-aft girder connecting ship's floor to the keel. **Kingpost** or **Sampson post** Post supporting derricks, usually in pairs and sometimes incorporating ventilators. **Goalpost masts** if pair joined by a horizontal bar. **Limbo** Mortar type depth-charge thrower. **Liner** Passenger or cargo vessel on regular service between ports. **Mack** Combined funnel and mast. **Magazine** Space for storing ammunition. **Mizzen** Third mast from bows or fishing vessel's aftermost mast. **Monkey Island** Platform above wheelhouse with extra binnacle. **Orlop** Lowermost deck of a warship or part deck which is not continuous. **Periscope** Long tube with arrangement of mirrors to enable submarine's officers to con surface of the sea while submerged. **Poop** Raised part of hull at the stern. **Porthole** Circular glazed 'window' in ship's side or superstructure plating. **Propeller** or **screw** Spiral blade driving mechanism. **Quarter deck** Aftermost deck of a warship or sailing ship reserved for officers or deck raised about half the normal height. **Radar** Electronic device for 'seeing' at night or in fog (*r*adio *det*ection *a*nd *r*anging). **Radome** Spherical protective shield for radar scanner. **Rudder** Flat vertical steering plate at ship's stern—sometimes additional rudder at the bows. **Run** Tapering part of ship's hull between parallel body and the stern. **Rubbing strake** Additional external length of wood running almost length of ship's sides to protect the hull from damage by quay-wall. **Sagging** Effect on hull when wave crests are at each end. **Seacat** Close range guided missile system for air defence. **Seaslug** Medium range missile system. **Seebee** Barge carrying vessel similar to LASH. **Screw** Propeller. **Scuttle** Glazed opening in hull or superstructure, or to sink a ship deliberately. **Scuppers** Openings to give deck drainage. **Sheerstrake** Uppermost line of plates on ship's side sometimes rounded at deck level. **Shelter deck** Deck above main deck usually with tonnage opening. **Soft-nosed stem** Rounded above water-line—often with company's emblem or badge. **Snort** Tube by which air is drawn into submarine while submerged. **Sonar** *So*und *N*avigation *A*nd *R*anging—underwater searching device like ASDIC. **Spanker** or driver, fore-and-aft gaff sail on aftermost mast of a sailing ship. **Spirket plate** Short section of bulwark on each side of forecastle at the stem. **Squid** Earlier type of mortar depth-charge thrower. **Stabilizers** Movable horizontal fins which can project from a ship's underwater hull to minimize rolling. **Stack** American term for funnel. **Stem** Foremost part of a ship's hull. **Stern** Aftermost part of the hull. **Stern tube** Long watertight steel tube in which the propeller shaft runs. **Strongback** Steel transverse hoop over a tug's after deck to protect deck fittings from tow rope. **Superstructure** Bridge, decks and deckhouses rising above ship's main structure—as distinct from islands which are part of it. **Topsides** Sides of hull between boot-topping and shelter deck level. **Tramp** A cargo vessel engaged in casual trade or on charter—not part of a regular service. **Triatic stay** Wire stay passing from truck of one mast to another. **Truck** Circular wooden cap at head of a mast with sheaves through which the signal halyards pass. **Turret** Totally enclosed and armoured rotating housing for one or more guns. **Turtleback** Forecastle with strongly curved sheerstrakes. **Tweendeck** Additional decks below main deck. **Wash ports** Freeing ports at foot of bulwarks for escape of excessive water. **Whaleback** Turtle-back forecastle of a fishing boat with working space beneath. **Well deck** Deck between two islands. **Winch** Steam, electric or hydraulic deck machinery for hoisting or hauling. **Windlass** Similar machine for hauling in anchor cable on forecastle.

INDEX OF SHIP TYPES

INDEX OF SHIP NAMES AND
CLASS DESIGNATIONS